Laundry day. Mrs. John Payzant washing clothes at the Wyman farm, Bon Accord, Alberta, circa 1915-1919 (Glenbow Archives, Calgary, Alberta [NA-2041-1]).

Life Writing Series / 4

Life Writing Series

In the **Life Writing Series,** Wilfrid Laurier University Press publishes life writing and new life-writing criticism in order to promote autobiographical accounts, diaries, letters and testimonials written and/or told by women and men whose political, literary or philosophical purposes are central to their lives. **Life Writing** features the accounts of ordinary people, written in English, or translated into English from French or the languages of the First Nations or from any of the languages of immigration to Canada. **Life Writing** will also publish original theoretical investigations about life writing, as long as they are not limited to one author or text.

Priority is given to manuscripts that provide access to those voices that have not traditionally had access to the publication process.

Manuscripts of social, cultural and historical interest that are considered for the series, but are not published, are maintained in the **Life Writing Archive** of Wilfrid Laurier University Library.

Series Editor
Marlene Kadar
Humanities Division, York University

Dear Editor and Friends
Letters from Rural Women of the North-West, 1900-1920

Norah L. Lewis, editor

Wilfrid Laurier University Press

This book has been published with the help of a grant in aid of publication from the Canada Council.

We acknowledge the financial support of the Government of Canada through the Book Publishing Industry Development Program for our publishing activities.

Canadian Cataloguing in Publication Data

Main entry under title:

   Dear editor and friends : letters from rural women of the North-West, 1900-1920

(Life writing ; 4)
Includes bibliographical references and index.
ISBN 0-88920-287-7

1. Rural women – Canada, Western – Correspondence.
2. Rural women – Canada, Northern – Correspondence.
3. Women pioneers – Canada, Western – Correspondence.
4. Women pioneers – Canada, Northern – Correspondence.
5. Canada, Western – Social life and customs – Sources.
6. Canada, Northern – Social life and customs – Sources.
I. Lewis, Norah Lillian, 1935- . II. Series.

HQ1453.D4 1998   305.4'09712'09041   C97-932474-2

Copyright © 1998
WILFRID LAURIER UNIVERSITY PRESS
Waterloo, Ontario, Canada   N2L 3C5

Cover design: Leslie Macredie
Cover photograph: Fishing at the Lower Falls on the Kootenay River, 1897 (West Kootenay Power Archives)

Printed in Canada

This book is dedicated to
three settler women of the North-West:

ALICE GRAYDON SULLIVAN (1867-1957)
LILLIAN TAYLOR WADDELL (1882-1953)
PEARL WADDELL-MCAUGHEY SULLIVAN (1903-1993)

Contents

Contents

List of Illustrations

Acknowledgments

I am grateful to Neil Sutherland and Jean Barman for their helpful suggestions and sage advice, to Linda Hale for her encouragement, and to Joyce McLean and Sharon Olding for their close reading of the letters. I also thank Margaret Whitehead and Jacqueline Gresko for their helpful comments and criticisms of the Introduction and the organization of the letters. A most sincere thank you to my husband Rolland Lewis for his help and patience with this project, and to Sandra Woolfrey for her encouragement and direction.

Thanks to the Delta Museum and Archives, The Glenbow Archives, The Provincial Archives of Manitoba, the Saskatchewan Archives Board, and the West Kootenay Power Archives for permission to reproduce photographs in this book.

This manuscript is the result of research conducted as part of the Canadian Childhood History Project, University of British Columbia, funded by a grant from the Social Sciences and Humanities Research Council of Canada.

The West Is Calling

I hear the wild West calling me;
The call rings sweet and clear
From woodland glades and mountains,
From silver lakes and fountains,
The haunts of fern and deer.

Oh the West has wondrous voices
Which sing a syren strain
So witchingly appealing
Through all the senses stealing
To lure one back again.

From the broad and willowy prairie,
The breezes waft the call;
Where the canyon hides its flowers,
Where the Rocky Summit towers,
It sounds at evening fall.

Where stars are glittering overhead,
And camp fires gleam around;
Where through the forest arches
The moose, unchallenged, marches,
And the wolves weird cries resound.

Oh the rapture of the wilds
In yonder wide wide West,
From the plains that without measure
Unroll their golden treasure,
To the purple mountain crest.

The West is waving welcome
To those who would be free
From the city's dust and clamor,
And by its subtle glamor,
The West has conquered me.

I pine to breathe again its air,
To scale the mountain side,
When the setting sun comes glinting
This foaming torrent tinting
Beyond the Great Divide!

MARY FRASER

Published in Woman's World, *Free Press Prairie Farmer*, July 11, 1906

Introduction

In 1902 my maternal grandparents, Lillian and Wesley Waddell, migrated from Parry Sound, Ontario, to a homestead in north-central Saskatchewan. Grandfather built a house and barn, cleared and seeded the land, and supplemented family income by working in lumber camps in the winter. Grandmother reared five daughters, planted gardens, raised poultry, milked cows, and spun and knitted wool from her own sheep. Although widowed in 1919 at age thirty-eight, she continued on the farm. Grandmother often talked about settlers' lack of accessible and adequate medical services, difficulties of travel, inadequate food and poor diets, isolation, widows left destitute, and the fate of families whose breadwinners suffered death, illnesses, loss of employment, or simply deserted. She supported the need for dower laws and women's rights. She treasured her right to vote and she voted in every election until her death in 1953. I regret that I did not ask her what hopes and dreams drew the family West. From where did she draw her strength to persevere in the face of terrible losses and setbacks? How did she cope with the silence and loneliness of the countryside? And if she had her life to live over, would she be a homesteader? As I read and selected the letters that follow, I realized how closely her life paralleled that of other women of the same time period, and I heard again the clear voice of my grandmother in chorus with thousands of settler women of the Canadian North-West.

Each time travellers cross the prairie provinces, sail along the isolated coast of British Columbia, or fly over the northern reaches of Vancouver Island, they see physical evidence of sites that once were homes, but are now long abandoned. The evidence may be weather-beaten, tumbled-down buildings, broken lines of fence posts, stands of trees that once served as windbreaks, derelict boats pulled up on lonely beaches or a

---

Notes to the Introduction are on pp. 14-17.

few rotting pilings of what was once a dock. Rusting machinery, bits of broken glass, scraps of furniture, and mortar and bricks from fallen chimneys confirm that people once lived here. Local residents may still refer to such sites by the names of the first homesteaders or original owners. They generally know the approximate year the settlers arrived and their ethnic or national origin, but little else about these long-gone residents. Such ruins are often the sole reminder of settlers who were part of the settlement and development of Western Canada.

Between 1891 and 1921 the population of the Canadian North-West increased from 348,600 to 2,793,000 residents, leading Winnipeg journalist James Gray to observe that the prairies were covered with a "seething mass of humanity seeking for a place on which to light."[1] Settlers, adventurers, and fortune seekers from other regions of Canada, the United States, Great Britain, Europe, Asia, and the Middle East flooded onto the prairies and into British Columbia, seeking free or cheap land, the hope of economic success, and religious and political freedom. The trans-Canada Canadian Pacific Railway (completed in 1886) and an increasing number of branch lines not only transported thousands of settlers into the West but also carried increasing quantities of high-quality milling wheat, lumber, fish, and minerals to eastern Canadian and overseas markets.[2]

With settlement came other developments. The 1891 North-West included the provinces of Manitoba and British Columbia and the vast Northwest Territories. The map of the North-West changed in 1898 when the Yukon Territory joined the Canadian federation, and again in 1905 when Alberta and Saskatchewan achieved provincial status. With the rapid settlement of the North-West and the growth of manufacturing centres in central Canada, it was little wonder Canada's political and economic leaders optimistically touted the twentieth century as "Canada's century."

Traditionally, historians have tended to examine the history of Canada in terms of political change and economic development. There is, however, more to the history of a nation or a region than politics and economics—there are the people who populated and developed the region. Only since the 1960s and 1970s have historians begun to examine and to analyze the lives and contributions of different socioeconomic classes or of specific ethnic, racial, or religious groups within a given time frame or a particular geographical area. As an example, reconstructing the history of any specific group, such as Western rural women, 1900 to 1920, presents several difficulties and challenges.

Historian Jane Errington observes that as women were seldom encouraged to record their lives and activities, researchers must seek historical
women through a wide range of both written and oral sources.[3] Furthermore, the reactions of one group of women are not necessarily common
to all women of the same time period or region. Nor can the customs
and actions of women of the past be interpreted in terms of present-day
values or attitudes. Consequently, in spite of all efforts, the voices of
some women will be still overlooked or unheard.

Settling the West

Women were in the minority in the North-West, although the ratio of
females to males varied by year, location, and ethnic group. But whether
indigenous residents or recent arrivals, women struggled to cope with
and to adapt to radical change. By 1900, for example, First Nations and
Metis women were experiencing the steady erosion of their traditional
culture and the breakdown of family and community ties. Many could
no longer follow their seasonal cycle of hunting, fishing, food gathering,
and preservation, and the world of many First Nations people was
restricted by the boundaries of their reserves.[4]

Settler women, most of whom arrived after 1880, generally came as
part of family groups or members of ethnic or religious settlement
groups, although a significant number of single, separated, or widowed
women came alone. They were a diverse group in terms of ethnic back-
ground, racial origin, social class, marital status, economic condition,
educational level, and religious affiliation. Few, however, were elderly.[5]
As newcomers, they faced the daunting tasks of establishing homes, rearing families, or finding employment to support themselves and, in some
cases, dependent children or aging or disabled relatives. Reports by government agents, health professionals, clergy, journalists, and travellers
indicate that life in rural areas was difficult and often tenuous. Further
insights into Western pioneer life are provided in recent collections of
photographs, tapes, and artifacts gathered for Canada's centennial year
(1967), provincial anniversaries, and community and school reunions. In
addition, aging Canadians who have preserved their personal recollec-
tions and family and community lore add to the growing body of historical information. Through this growing body of information it becomes
increasingly apparent that women were not only participants in but also
makers of history. Their contributions to pioneer life were acknowl-
edged as early as 1905 by Manitoba pioneer Mr. W. Fulton in his

address to the Portage la Prairie Old Timers meeting. Pioneer women, he observed, were central to the settlement process and to the development of communities. They were the ones who brought culture, hospitality, intellectual thought, morality, and compassion to those in need.[6]

Another significant and valuable window into rural settler life is provided through letters written to the women's pages of agricultural publications such as the Montreal-published *Family Herald and Weekly Star* (1869-1968), the Winnipeg-published *Free Press Prairie Farmer* (1872-1968), *The Farmer's Advocate* (1866-1965), *Grain Growers' Guide* (1908-1963), *Western Home Monthly* (1904-1950), and the Saskatoon-published *Saturday Press and Prairie Farm* (1909-1917). In their letters we hear the clear, authentic voices of real women who lived on homesteads and ranches, in logging and mining camps, in fishing communities, and along traplines somewhere between the Manitoba-Ontario border and Vancouver Island. Many rural families, including immigrant families, subscribed to one or more of these publications because such papers carried a wide range of national and international news, information of interest to agriculturalists, the commodities markets, medical and legal advice, suggestions for food preparation and preservation, recreational reading, and handicraft activities for both adults and children. Once read, newspapers were generally passed on to friends and neighbours.[7]

In selecting the letters that follow, I examined hundreds of letters in all available issues (on microfilm) of the *Free Press Prairie Farmer* and *The Farmer's Advocate*, 1900 to 1920, six months for each year of the *Family Herald and Weekly Star*, 1900 to 1920, all available issues of the *Grain Growers' Guide*, 1908 to 1920, and the *Western Home Monthly*, 1904 to 1914, and four issues of the *Saturday Press and Prairie Farm*, 1916 -1917. I selected these letters because they were representative of the experiences and challenges faced by rural women of the North-West—isolation, loneliness, a lack of traditional support networks, and the need for changes that gave women and their dependent children both personal and property rights. Other letters were included because they were instructive, amusing, informative, or addressed specific events or conditions that touched the families or communities of letter writers. I also attempted to select letters that represented writers from a variety of ethnic backgrounds and geographical locations, and related the physical, intellectual, and emotional responses by both newcomers and long-time residents to rural life. A number of letters were included because they described the generosity and support demonstrated by some and the intolerance and prejudice shown by others. I made a conscious attempt to give readers a broad view rather than a narrow focus on rural pioneer life.

The Role of Women

Although diverse, letter writers were a select group in that they were motivated to write and sufficiently literate in English to do so, though their literacy skills varied greatly. Several women enlisted others to write their letters for them. Writers rarely gave their names or postal addresses, but rather used pseudonyms that revealed much about their mental, emotional, or economic conditions, sense of humour, occupations, ethnic roots, or religious faith. The headings or titles of the letters were added by editors and generally reflected either the content of the letter or an issue raised by the writer. Editors kept records of the names and addresses of letter writers. Although many readers stated their ethnic origins or regional roots, no writers indicated they were First Nations or Metis women. (As several First Nations children wrote to the children's pages of these same newspapers, their mothers may also have written to the women's pages.) There were a number of letters from male readers commenting on women's issues, offering "interesting" housekeeping hints, or seeking housekeepers or spouses. Missing, however, were the voices of those not yet literate in English, many non-subscribers, the very poor, and those not motivated to write.

Many women came willingly to the North-West, sharing their husbands' vision of Utopia and swayed by prevalent and pervasive propaganda that ensured success—if they worked hard. Others came reluctantly, out of duty to husbands or fathers. As letter writer Marie told fellow readers, "we must leave all behind, and go where stern duty bids us." But the West was not the Garden of Eden portrayed by propaganda materials and land company agents, and many settlers were unprepared by experience, training, or temperament for the physical, financial, and emotional demands of pioneer life. Those unwilling or unable to adapt were either trapped in a cycle of misery and poverty or else moved on in the hope of better luck in new places.[8]

Women who wished to take up homesteads found that under the terms of the *Dominion Land Act*, 1872, only adult males and women who were sole heads of households, such as widows with young families, could make application for (file for) 160 acres of unalienated (homestead) land. Homesteaders paid a small fee at the local land office to cover the legal cost of registering a specific quarter section. Homesteaders did not get clear title to their land until they had completed specified developments that included a shack or house, a stable, and a set number of acres cleared and seeded to crop. Women were permitted to buy farm land and many of them did so. Unattached women were expected to marry, help make the family enterprise successful, produce a family, and thus fulfil their role in the settlement of the West. As Eliane Leslau Silverman noted, women were expected to marry for economic rather than romantic reasons.[9]

Most women on their own, particularly those with little education or no specific training useful in a pioneer community, were employed as domestic workers by busy farm or ranch wives. Domestic workers, many of whom were immigrants, were generally unprepared for the heavy work, long hours, and diversity of tasks demanded of them. They complained that farm women treated them little better than slaves. On the other hand, their employers countered that domestic workers were incompetent, lazy, and more interested in finding husbands than in doing a good day's work. There was, however, a discrepancy between what rural women expected of their domestic help and what they wanted for their daughters. Many rural parents encouraged their daughters to train as nurses or teachers, as both professions offered financial independence and an escape from the drudgery and monotony of farm life.[10]

There is no doubt that life on the frontier was difficult and demanding. As had settler women in seventeenth- and eighteenth-century New France, the Maritimes, and Ontario, settler women of the North-West were "required to perform superhuman feats of endurance, courage, and household skills as they faced the difficulties inherent in the settling of an often hostile physical environment."[11] For many there was a blurring of what, in their own culture, were traditional gender roles. Letter writers agreed that looking after their families, houses, gardens, poultry, and dairies was women's work, but for some working in the field or looking after livestock was a new responsibility. Others reported that their skills as hunters, fishers, and trappers supplemented the family larder and income and kept animal predators from taking their poultry and killing young livestock. In many settler families, husbands worked away from home in logging, fishing, construction, or as farm labourers, leaving wives and children to manage and operate the family enterprise for months at a time. There is little doubt that the success of many settlers was the result of the combined efforts, dedication, and hard work of all members of the family.[12]

Because of their contribution to the family business, many farm women considered themselves partners with their husbands, both in the division of labour and in decision making. Many husbands appeared to share that view. But other women reported that they had no voice in the operation, management, or income of the family enterprise. As Rasmussen et al. observed, there were married women who had the responsibilities of adults but no legal status or rights as wives. By law a married woman had the right to manage her own money and property as if she were single, but most women had neither money nor property. But a married women who worked to develop the family farm, ranch, or business was not legally entitled to any share of the family enterprise either while her husband was living or after his death. Furthermore, a husband could sell, mortgage, or rent the family enterprise without his wife's consent or even her knowledge if it was registered in the husband's name; a wife could thus be left homeless and penniless with children to rear. In addition, the father was the sole legal guardian of underage children, and until such time as the children were of age, he could, without the mother's consent, plan the children's education, put them up for adoption, or arrange for a third party to become their guardian.[13] As early as 1905, women in Western Canada began to agitate for dower laws, but not until 1920 had all four Western provinces enacted laws that ensured both the personal and property rights of wives and dependent children.

The Need to Connect

Why did women write to the women's pages? What need or whim drove them to share personal concerns and expose their vulnerability to strangers? Although their letters touched on many topics, writers tended to focus on four major themes: their desire to share recent adventures and experiences with others; their loneliness and isolation; their lack of traditional support groups and networks; and the need for laws to protect their own personal and property rights and those of their children.

For many, emigrating and homesteading was the most exciting and important event of their lives, and they wrote to share their adventures. Others wrote to fulfill a creative urge and newspapers provided one outlet. They described the vista of prairie or mountain they saw from their windows. They reported the arrival of more settlers, the coming of the railroad, the opening of schools and churches, the formation of community organizations and associations, and they encouraged others to come West.

But beauty and progress were not enough to relieve their loneliness. The systematic surveying of the prairies into sections and quarter sections, and the scattering of settlers along British Columbia's rugged coastline and interior valleys meant long, empty distances between settlers. Those settlers who came from urban centres or lived in small villages central to community fields and pastures found the vast, sparsely populated expanse of prairie landscape overwhelming. Others felt stifled in an isolated cabin surrounded by water, forest, or mountains. To visit a neighbour or to go to town required walking long distances, driving horses or oxen over inadequate roads, or travelling by boat. Although there were women who travelled extensively with their husbands, most, particularly those with young children, opted to stay home rather than endure a long, rough trip in winter cold or summer heat. Furthermore, someone had to milk the cows, feed the livestock, and keep the home fires burning.

Settler women were often as isolated by language, religion, ethnic origin, or deep-rooted prejudices as they were by distance, yet they needed practical advice about childrearing, poultry raising, and butter making as well as someone to comfort them at the deaths of their children or husbands, or the loss of their flocks, herds, gardens, and crops. For many, the women's pages partially filled that need. One woman reported that as she never received personal mail she considered the weekly women's pages to be letters from friends. Several others described the arrival of the weekly women's page as being akin to a visit with friends or having a house full of visitors. As a young teacher in Snowshoe, British Columbia, Marjorie Thatcher recalled that the Home Loving Hearts page was important to lonely farm women. She observed that it helped keep them "from climbing the walls" of their shacks.[14]

Isolation based on prejudice was common and overt. Not only did immigrants and migrants bring centuries-old antagonisms with them, but the pressure of so many newcomers created new tensions. A few letter writers named those nationalities they deemed acceptable, tolerable, and contemptible. On the reverse side, other women related situations in which they were treated with contempt, scorn, or open hostility by employers, neighbours, and fellow travellers. Isolation, whether physical, social, or emotional, took its toll. Lonely women frequently experienced deteriorating health, poor self-images, marital stresses, and serious depressions. There were, of course, positive aspects to isolation. Out of necessity, isolation fostered self-sufficiency in individuals and the need for and advantages of cooperation among settlers—a factor that would shape the political, economic, and social development in the West. Canadian writer George Woodcock suggested that isolation "produced a breed of thoughtful individuals."[15] Perhaps that was true—if individuals survived the loneliness.

Isolated women were also deprived of the close, trusting relationships, practical advice, companionship, and consolation they normally received from traditional support networks such as their mothers and older women, their peer group, and religious and cultural associations. In 1890, Minnie May, women's editor for the *The Farmer's Advocate* summed it up: "In all our trials women's greatest friend should be women. It is the very greatest comfort to have a woman friend to whom one can turn for consolation when all seems dark around us, and she can say the words you most want to hear."[16]

But women were pragmatists. They recognized their own strengths and limitations and utilized their own meagre resources. They quickly determined which neighbours gave wise advice, helped during childbirth, or assisted at a barn raising. But developing new support networks took time, and rural women had little time to spare.[17]

For many, the women's pages provided a vital support network based on a trust relationship between female editors, letter writers, and readers. Editors usually responded with compassion, encouragement, and suggestions as to where and from whom readers could seek advice or assistance. With small contributions from readers (ranging from a few pennies to a few dollars), Lilly Emily F. Barry [Hostess], editor of the *Family Herald and Weekly Star*'s Circle of Good Company (1896 to 1905) and Margaret Shields, conductor (not editor) of the *Grain Growers' Guide*'s Sunshine Guild, provided layettes, children's clothing, toys and books for needy families. Barry required a letter from the local postmaster, clergyman, or government official confirming a family was in need. As editors recorded the names and addresses of letter writers, they were able to forward clothing, bedding, quilt patches, garden seed, plant roots, reading materials, and in a few cases money, from those willing to share to those in dire need. But as generous as readers were, they were also quick to pour scorn upon any they deemed untruthful, immoral, lazy, or wasteful, or with whom they disagreed on political, racial, or religious issues.[18]

While some conditions could be eased if not solved by advice and generosity, others could not. A growing number of women's groups, including Homemaker Clubs, Women's Institutes, Women Grain Growers, United Farm Women of Alberta, United Farm Women of Manitoba,

Women's Christian Temperance Union (WCTU), Political Equality League, Local Councils of Women, and the Canadian Women's Press Club, were dedicated to improving conditions, not only for women but also for families and society in general. Each organization tended to focus on specific but often interrelated issues such as dower laws, property rights, guardianship of children, moral reform, prohibition, improved and expanded educational facilities, accessible medical care and health services, better working and living conditions, and for some, birth control information. Women recognized that without suffrage they lacked the power to effect change; for women of the North-West, suffrage was not an end in itself, but rather a means to an end.

Support for women's suffrage was certainly not unanimous, but as Carol Bacchi's study indicates, agricultural associations and organized labour generally supported women's demand for suffrage.[19] Western women also received encouragement and direction from three other interconnected groups—the leadership of women's organizations, feminist reformers, and female editors. Through their newspaper columns, female editors reached into the homes of thousands of rural Western women on a weekly or biweekly basis. Many readers regarded them as friends and confidants, and thus tended to trust their advice.

New Brunswick-born writer Kate Simpson Hayes [Mary Markwell], first female journalist in the West and founding member of the Canadian Women's Press Club, worked at the Manitoba *Free Press* from 1899-1906. Hayes set the pattern when she focused the contents of the women's page on the concerns of Western Canadian readers: child and family health; food preparation and preservation; sewing patterns and knitting instructions; and news of women's groups across Canada and around the world. Her successor, Lillian Beynon Thomas [Lillian Laurie], editor of the women's page from 1906-1917, was an appropriate choice. Thomas, farm-born and reared, had served as a field worker and organizer of Homemaker Clubs for the University of Saskatchewan Extension Branch, and she was a founding member of the Manitoba Political Equality League. Thomas formed the Mutual Benefit Association (M.B.A.) through which readers of and letter writers to the Home Loving Hearts pages encouraged one another, shared information, and exchanged ideas and materials. Thomas worked closely with feminist reformers, including Nellie McClung and columnist E. Cora Hind, in their campaign for women's suffrage and women's rights. She used her weekly column to encourage women to organize, to hold public meetings, to conduct letter writing campaigns, and to present petitions to political leaders demanding dower laws, guardianship of their children, and suffrage.[20]

Thomas' colleague E. Cora Hind, commercial and agricultural columnist for the *Free Press* from 1901-1930, was respected for her knowledge of farm life, her accuracy in crop forecasts and harvest predictions, and her success in extending export markets for Canadian farm products. In addition, she regularly contributed articles to the weekly women's page. Hind recognized that flourishing family enterprises would lead to an improvement in farm and family life. Hind was active in the WCTU, an advocate of better conditions in women's jails, a member of the Manitoba Equal Franchise Club, and along with Thomas, a participant in the campaign by the Manitoba Political Equality League that led to women's suffrage.[21]

A fourth outstanding female journalist and advocate of women's rights was Francis Marion Beynon, editor of The Country Homemakers page of the *Grain Growers' Guide*, 1912-1917, and sister to Lillian Beynon Thomas. A political activist and a member of the Political Equality League and the Canadian Press Club, Beynon was a dedicated suffragist working for a newspaper that was pro-suffrage. Beynon insisted upon universal female suffrage, not only for Canadian and British women or those whose relatives were in the military, but also for foreign-born and recent immigrant women. Women, Beynon insisted, should stand on their own feet, and marriage should be a partnership in which responsibility and success were shared. As a journalist, she stimulated interest in the activities of women's organizations and encouraged women to agitate and work for suffrage. Beynon, Thomas, and Thomas' husband, Vernon Thomas, were pacifists, but pacifism was an unpopular stance in the midst of the First World War (1914-1918). In 1917 they moved to the United States, but not before Lillian Thomas and Francis Beynon made major contributions to the fight for women's rights.[22]

British-born Violet MacNaughton, teacher, social worker, founding president of the Saskatchewan Women Grain Growers (1913), and first president of the Saskatchewan Equal Franchise League (later the Political Equality League), was at the forefront of political activism for many years. MacNaughton advocated suffrage for women, but she saw many other needs as well. She pushed for the development of public health nursing services and community libraries, and she supported the immigration of large numbers of domestics from Britain and Europe to help busy farm and ranch wives. As the editor of Our Welfare Page of the *Saturday Press and Prairie Farm*, 1916-1917, and the first editor of the women's page of the *The Western Producer*, 1925-1950, MacNaughton addressed a broad range of other issues, including agricultural economics, farm movement solidarity, co-operative associations, world peace, multiculturalism and immigration, and improved health, education, and social services for children.[23]

All five editors understood the problems faced by rural women. They treated their readers with respect and compassion. Through their columns they were able to reach large numbers of rural women and to encourage readers to campaign for change. The advice and suggestions editors gave were practical and workable, thereby enabling rural women to feel that they, along with other feminist reformers, had done their part to achieve suffrage, prohibition, and increased health and education services.

In British Columbia, demands for women's suffrage began in the 1880s. Women were permitted to vote in school board elections in 1895 and municipal elections in 1906; however, the right to vote in municipal elections was rescinded in 1907. Women did not achieve suffrage in provincial and federal elections until 1917. The Women's Institute, organized in British Columbia in 1909, focused on improving life in rural homes and communities, but appeared not to play a major role in the suffrage movement, although individual members, including Mrs. V. S. MacLachlan, the first superintendent of the Institute in British Columbia, and Elizabeth Roberts MacDonald of Nelson both campaigned for women's suffrage. On the other hand, Cecilia Spofford, Helen Gregory McGill, and Maria Gordon Grant led the membership of the WCTU, the Local Council of Women, and the Political Equality League in the struggle for women's suffrage.[24]

Changes came slowly at first, and not at the same rate in all provinces. The *Alberta Married Women's Relief Act*, 1910, guaranteed widows a share of their husbands' estates. The *Saskatchewan Homestead Act*, 1915, gave Saskatchewan wives the right to prevent the sale or mortgage of the home quarter without their signatures, and the *Devolution of Estates Act* of 1919 guaranteed widows from 33 to 100 percent of their husbands' estates, depending on the size of their family. The *Infants Act*, 1920, made the mothers the usual guardian of children under fourteen years of age. The *Alberta Intestate Succession Act* of 1920 and the *Manitoba Dower Act* of 1918 assured that wives could not be left homeless or totally disinherited. British Columbia was the first province to enact equal child guardianship and custody laws in 1920. By 1920, wives in the four Western provinces had a measure of control over family property, and husbands could not legally leave wives homeless and penniless.[25]

Suffrage in provincial elections was achieved in Manitoba, Saskatchewan, and Alberta in 1916, and in British Columbia in 1917. In 1917, the federal government extended the franchise to military nurses and close relatives of military personnel, and in 1918 to women over the age of twenty-one. (There were exclusions, however, including Aboriginals and Asians.) With the support of women's votes, between 1915 and 1917, all provinces in Canada except Quebec enacted laws establishing prohibition against the sale of alcohol. In February 1918, nation-wide prohibition was establish for the duration of the war and one year thereafter.[26] Over the next few years, prohibition laws were slowly but surely repealed.

The First World War (1914-1918) also brought major changes to rural life. Men rushed to enlist, leaving wives and children to do the plowing, seeding, haying, and harvesting. Farm labour was in short supply, and the only available males were either too young or too old to enlist, unfit for military service, or immigrants from enemy countries. Letter writers berated those who did not enlist as slackers." They particularly resented "foreigners" who demanded higher wages than their husbands or brothers received while fighting for King and country.[27]

But the war also provided an opportunity for young people to move into shop, office, and factory jobs previously held by men. For many, it was an interesting and satisfying experience. But when the war ended factories closed down, soldiers returned expecting jobs, and wartime workers were laid off. Because these wartime workers had low educational levels and no specific trade or skill, many were trapped in a lifetime of low-paid manual labour.[28]

Those on the home front did their bit to win the war. Urban youngsters were recruited to work on farms and in orchards and truck gardens. Entire communities raised money for the war effort, the Patriotic Fund, and the Red Cross. Adults and children knitted socks, mitts, and balaclavas, rolled bandages, and packed parcels for soldiers. But the war also sparked a wide range of highly charged emotions—pride, anger, prejudice, hostility, and sorrow. Women were appalled at the number of illegitimate "war babies," but divided as to whether women or soldiers were at fault. They were bitter and sorrowful when those they knew and loved were listed among the wounded, missing, or dead. Family circles were broken, whole communities drained of their young men and future leaders, and Canadian society was irrevocably changed by the First World War.[29]

Canadian participation in the war, however, was only one factor that changed rural life in the North-West. With settlement and development came expanded rail and road systems and a proliferation of villages and hamlets serving surrounding rural areas. For those who could afford them, telephones were a priority and motor cars and trucks were common. Medical, education, and religious services and facilities were vastly improved. Active agricultural associations and women's organizations focused the efforts of their membership on improving rural life. In spite of these changes, letter writers indicated that the daily cycle of chores and the seasonal cycle of tasks continued to control their lives. Women not only partook in but they also created history in Canada's North-West.

Notes

1 James H. Gray, *The Roar of the Twenties* (Markham: Paperjacks, 1982), 5.

2 Ramsay Cook, "The Triumphs and Trials of Materialism 1900-1945," in *The Illustrated History of Canada*, ed. Craig Brown (Toronto: Lester and Orpen Dennys, 1987), 383-84; David K. Foote, *Canada's Population Outlook: Demographic Futures and Economic Challenges* (Toronto: Lorimer, 1982), 12, Table 1-3. Yukon and Northwest Territories are included in the 1921 population numbers.

3 Jane Errington, "Pioneers and Suffragists," in *Changing Patterns: Women in Canada*, ed. Sandra Burt, Lorraine Code, and Lindsey Dorney (Toronto: McClelland and Stewart, 1988), 51-78.

4 Foote, *Canada's Population Outlook*, Table 1-6: Sex Ratios for Canada and the Provinces, 1901-1981; Olive Patricia Dickason, *Canada's First Nations: A History of Founding Peoples from Earliest Times* (Toronto: McClelland and Stewart, 1992); Donald Purich, *The Metis* (Toronto: Lorimer, 1988), 9-13.

5 Alan B. Anderson, "Ethnic Identity in Saskatchewan Bloc Settlements: A Sociological Appraisal," in *The Settlement of the West*, ed. Howard Palmer (Calgary: University of Calgary, 1977), 188-93; Lynne Bowen, *Muddling Through: The Remarkable Story of the Barr Colonists* (Vancouver: Douglas and McIntyre, 1992); R. Douglas Francis, *Images of the West: Responses to the Canadian Prairies* (Saskatoon: Western Producer Prairie Books, 1989), 109-10; Jean Barman, *The West Beyond the West: A History of British Columbia* (Toronto: University of Toronto Press, 1991), 129-50.

6 When Alberta and Saskatchewan celebrated their seventy-fifth anniversaries as provinces in 1980, dozens of Western communities produced fine local histories: Susan Jackel, *A Flannel Shirt and Liberty: British Emigrant Gentlewomen in the Canadian West, 1880-1914* (Vancouver: University of British Columbia

Press, 1982), xviii, xxii-xxiii; Jaroslav Petryshyn, *Peasants in the Promised Land: Canada and the Ukrainians* (Toronto: Lorimer, 1985), 74-82; Mary E. Inderwick, "A Lady and Her Ranch," in *The Best from Alberta History*, ed. Hugh Dempsey (Saskatoon: Western Producer Prairie Books, 1981), 65-77; "Women of the West," *Grain Growers' Guide*, June 5, 1905.

7 In 1917, the *Family Herald and Weekly Star*, *Free Press Pairie Farmer*, and the *Farmer's Advocate* had a total of 253,671 subscribers. There were an additional 33,657 subscribers to the *Grain Growers' Guide*. The previous year (1916) the *Western Home Monthly* reported approximately 44,000 subscribers and the *Saturday Press and Prairie Farm* 4,500 subscribers. Yearly subscriptions were $1.00 for the *Family Herald and Weekly Star* and *Free Press Prairie Farmer*, $1.50 for the *Farmer's Advocate* and *Grain Growers' Guide*, and $2.00 for the *Western Home Monthly* (Walter Wicks, *Memories of the Skeena* [Saanichton: Hancock Press, 1976], 26). Vancouver resident Lena Rogolsky reported that the *Family Herald and Weekly Star* was a popular publication in her immigrant parents' Russian-speaking home (Violet MacNaughton Papers: Saskatchewan Archives Board, Regina).

8 *Women's Work in Western Canada*, issued by the Canadian Pacific Railway Company, 1906. Pamphlet No. 9: Ontario Archives; "Marie," *Free Press Prairie Farmer*, February 6, 1907; Anna B. Woywitka, "A Struggle for Survival," *Alberta History* 37 (Summer 1989), 1-25; Harry Pinuta, *Land of Pain: Land of Promise* (Saskatoon: Western Producer Prairie Books, 1978), Preface.

9 *Women of Canada: Their Life and Work* (N.p.: National Council of Women, 1900), 34-40; Eliane Leslau Silverman, "Women's Perception of Marriage on the Alberta Frontier," in *Building Beyond the Homestead*, ed. David C. Jones and Ian MacPherson (Calgary: University of Calgary, 1985), 49; J. E. Conway, *The West: A History of a Region in Confederation* (Toronto: Lorimer, 1994), 26-32. The failure rate of homesteaders was very high. Between 1870 and 1927, on a national basis 40 percent of free homesteads failed; in Alberta, 1905 to 1936, 46 percent failed, and in Saskatchewan, 1911 to 1931, 57 percent failed.

10 Approximately 67,000 domestic workers entered Canada between 1909 and 1914, but not all moved to the North-West (Candace Savage, "domestic service," in *Foremothers* [Saskatoon: N.p., 1975], 15: Saskatchewan Archives Board). Savage quotes from a pamphlet issued by the Department of the Interior, entitled "Women's Work in Canada," 1915; Georgina Binnie Clark, *Wheat and Women* (Toronto: Bell and Cockburn, 1914); Robert S. Patterson, "Voices from the Past: The Personal and Professional Struggle of Rural School Teachers," in *Schools in the West: Essays in Canadian Educational History*, ed. Nancy M. Sheehan, J. Donald Wilson, and David C. Jones (Calgary: Detselig, 1986), 99-111.

11 Elizabeth Thompson, *The Pioneer Women* (Montreal: McGill-Queen's University Press, 1991), 60; Jacqueline Bliss, "Seamless Lives: Pioneer Women of Saskatoon 1883-1903," *Saskatchewan History* 43 (August 1992), 84-100.

12 Errington, "Pioneers and Suffragists, 51-79.

13 Linda Rasmussen et al., eds., *A Harvest Yet to Reap* (Toronto: The Women's Press, 1976), 42; Veronica Strong-Boag, "Pulling in Double Harness or Hauling a Double Load: Women, Work and Feminism on the Canadian Prairie," *Journal of Canadian Studies* 21 (Autumn 1986), 32-52; Alison Prentice et al., *Canadian Women: A History* (Toronto: Harcourt Brace Jovanovich, 1988), 120; *Women of Canada*, 34-40; Savage, *Foremothers*, i-iv, 39-41; Barman, *The West Beyond the West*, 202-204, 210-11, 225. The money women earned from selling eggs, cream, and butter was generally considered their "pin money," but in many cases it was the only money to come into the house for months at a time and many women used it to run the household.

14 John MacDougall, *Rural Life in Canada: Its Trends and Tasks* (Toronto: University of Toronto Press, 1973; originally published in 1913), 36; Farmer's Helper, *Free Press Prairie Farmer*, April 6, 1910; Ontario, in ibid., July 8, 1908; Lee, in ibid.

15 J. S. Woodsworth, *Strangers within Our Gates* (Toronto: University of Toronto Press, 1972; originally published in 1909), 161-67. Woodsworth's study pointed out the problems created by mass immigration for both immigrants and communities. Georgina M. Taylor, " 'Shall I Drown Myself Now or Later?' The Isolation of Rural Women in Saskatchewan and Their Participation in the Homemakers' Clubs, the Farm Movement and the Co-operative Commonwealth Federation 1910-1967," in *Women: Isolation and Bonding— The Ecology of Gender*, ed. Kathleen Storrie (London: Methuen, 1987), 79-100; Lillian Laurie, in *Free Press Prairie Farmer*, February 27, 1907; George Woodcock, *A Social History of Canada* (Toronto: Penguin, 1988), 285.

16 "Minnie May," *Farmer's Advocate*, August 1890; Anna B. Woywitka, "A Roumanian Pioneer," in Dempsey, *The Best from Alberta*, 130-39.

17 Rasmussen, *A Harvest Yet to Reap*, 122-23; Mary Hallett and Marilyn Davis, *Firing the Heather: The Life and Times of Nellie McClung* (Saskatoon: Fifth House, 1993), 102-47; Prentice et al., *Canadian Women*, 114-20. A poignant example of the need for support was shown in Laurie's column Home Loving Hearts, *Free Press Prairie Farmer*, March 26, 1913. An elderly women had come to Saskatchewan to keep house for her son. He treated her brutally, but she was afraid to tell anyone. She wrote Laurie to ask if anyone would be willing to pay her fare and give her a small wage if she would come work for them. Several readers quickly offered to do so, but the woman did not contact Laurie again.

18 Nanci Langford and Norah Keating, "Social Isolation and Alberta Farm Women," in *Women: Isolation and Bonding*, 47-53; Angus McLaren and Arleen Tiger McLaren, *The Bedroom and the State: The Changing Practices of Contraception and Abortion in Canada, 1880-1980* (Toronto: McClelland and Stewart, 1986), 9-53; Norah L. Lewis, "Goose Grease and Turpentine: Mother Treats the Family's Illnesses," *Prairie Forum* 13, (Spring 1990): 79. The dissemination of birth control information was illegal, but readers appeared to share what little they knew. For example, "Snow Bird," *Free*

Press Prairie Farmer, May 8, 1929: "Snow Bird" complained that she had used squaw vine as recommended by "Young Manitoba," but it was unsuccessful and she was pregnant.

19 Carol Bacchi, "Divided Allegiances: The Response of Farm and Labour Women to Suffrage," in *A Not Unreasonable Claim: Women and Reform in Canada 1880s-1920s*, ed. Linda Kealey (Toronto: Canadian Women's Educational Press, 1979), 89-108; Savage, *Foremothers*, i-iv, 61-65.

20 Paul Voicey, "The 'Votes for Women' Movement," in Dempsey, *The Best from Alberta History*, 166-201; Kay Rex, *No Daughter of Mine: The Women and History of the Canadian Women's Press Club 1904-1971* (Toronto: Cedar Cave, 1995), 1-22; Savage, *Foremothers*, 19-20, 24-25.

21 Kay, *No Daughter of Mine*, 3-6; Deborah Gorham, "The Canadian Suffragists," in *Women in the Canadian Mosaic*, ed. Gwen Matheson (Toronto: Peter Martin, 1976), 23-55.

22 Savage, *Foremothers*, 1-3; Prentice et al., *Canadian Women*, 197, 207; Rasmussen, *A Harvest Yet to Reap*, 88-89, 122-23.

23 R. G. Marchildon, "Improving the Quality of Rural Life in Saskatchewan: Activities of the Women's Section of the Saskatchewan Grain Growers," in *Building Beyond the Homestead*, ed. David C. Jones and Ian MacPherson (Calgary: University of Calgary, 1985), 89-110.

24 Errington, "Pioneers and Suffragists," 69-77; Barman, *The West Beyond the West*, 214-15, 218-20; Michael H. Cramer, "Public and Political: Documents of the Woman's Suffrage Campaign in British Columbia, 1871-1917: The View from Victoria," in *British Columbia Reconsidered: Essays on Women*, ed. Gillian Creese and Veronica Strong-Boag (Vancouver: Press Gang Publishers, 1992), 55 -69.

25 Margaret MacLellan, "History of Women's Rights in Canada," in *Cultural Tradition and Political History of Women in Canada*, Study No. 8 of the Royal Commission on the Status of Women (Ottawa, 1971), 4, 15-16; Hallett and Davis, *Firing the Heather*, 147; Prentice et al., *Canadian Women*, 207-10; Barman, *The West Beyond the West*, 225.

26 John Herd Thompson, *The Harvests of War: The Prairie West, 1914-1918* (Toronto: McClelland and Stewart, 1978), 22-27, 73-94.

27 Norah L. Lewis, " 'Isn't this a terrible war?': The Attitudes of Children to Two World Wars," *Historical Studies in Education/Revue d'histoire de l'éducation* 7 (Fall 1995): 193-215; James H. Gray, *The Boy from Winnipeg* (Toronto: Macmillan, 1970), 86-96; Gray, *The Roar of the Twenties*, 42-52.

28 Ibid., 213-15.

29 Ibid.

Letters from Rural Women of the North-West, 1900-1920

CIRCLE OF GOOD COMPANY, *Family Herald and Weekly Star*
December 20, 1899

Dear Hostess:

Will you kindly permit an Outlander to join your charming circle? But please do not laugh, G.C., if my English is a little bit crude. I am only eighteen years old, and trying to improve it, if slowly, because I have very little time, being a farmer's daughter, with plenty of work to do.

My father takes the Family Herald and Weekly Star, and we like it very much. Now, I always read the war news first, for I know no rest till I have seen how the British are getting on in the war with the Boers. I hope they will be victorious; indeed, I can not believe it will be otherwise.

I am unlike my forefathers (the Vikings), who liked nothing better than warfare, for I am wishing the nations would settle their quarrels by other methods than these dreadful wars.

Will you please tell me, dear Hostess, whether stenography can be successfully learned at home, by the correspondence method, as some schools offer to teach by? I enclose a two-cent stamp for a book, please send me "Lorna Doone," if you have it in the library?

With all good wishes to you and G.C.

Manitoba   ICELANDER

Icelander's English is by no means crude. I hope she will write again. Will not some of the stenographers in the Circle correspond with Icelander and give her the desired information? I doubt if one could become an expert stenographer by studying without a teacher, though undoubtedly great headway can be made by private study and practice.

GOOD COMPANY, *Family Herald and Weekly Star*
February 28, 1900

Dear Hostess:

I live near the lovely Turtle Mountains of Manitoba. In the summer they are beautifully dressed in living green, the wild morning glories climb and trail over every shrub and bush, but alas! they are all gray now. The wild hops are so thick one can hardly climb through the flowers, hundreds of different kinds. The prairie was very lovely last summer. I am very fond of the orange lilies. They are like soldiers standing ready for battle in all their glory. The winter is very mild here, hardly snow enough for sleighing. My favourite poem is Longfellow. I never tire reading his poems. Don't you love him, too, mine Hostess? I am very fond of music. I can play a little on the violin and piano. I am also fond of reading and painting. Of course, I find plenty of other work to do, and I like any kind of work, even tending horses, being passionately fond of them. I have some reading matter I could send to someone who would like it.

Manitoba   TOM BOY

GOOD COMPANY, *Family Herald and Weekly Star*
April 4, 1900

Dear Hostess:

I am a farmer's wife, living in East Assiniboia, in the far-famed Moose Mountain country. I came here from Ontario nearly eighteen years ago with a small family; neighbours were few and far between. How often in the first year, I longed for a sight of some of my friends and old neighbours, no one but my Maker and myself know. Imagine being sixty miles from a Post Office for over a year! We had church, but no schools for a long time. But hope, grit, and work, will do wonders sometimes. Now the country will soon be filled up, and neighbours are close to each other. There are schools all over, we have everything we need but a railway, and it is nearly in sight; we expect it through here in early summer. We have a vast country and it is rightly called the garden of the North-West; it is a prairie with beautiful bluffs starting up here and there. The Moose Mountains are not high, they consist of hay meadows, lovely little lakes, bluffs, sloughs, and bush. There is a larger lake called Fish Lake, with lots of fish in it; in the summer people come from a distance of one hundred and forty miles for an outing, fishing, boating, and berry picking. There are two Indian Reserves in the mountains. The red men are getting civilized now. Dear Hostess, how I enjoyed the motto for the week and your weekly talks, and the letters of the company! How many uplifting thoughts and helps for the home. How sad it is that so many noble lives are lost on the African plains; how many desolate homes, heart broken mothers, and vacant chairs will be left! So many of our own Canadians that went so nobly will never come back! I hope the war will soon be over.

I could send Sabbath school papers and other reading matter to the needy if I had their addresses. I noticed in August 30th of last year, Nita, Gaspe, a shut-in requesting reading material. If I had her address I would write to her and send her reading if she would like it; also to Hetty, of Manitoba, or any other needy one. I would like Hertha, of Gaspe, to write to me. I have been acquainted with Weary Mother for a long time, we very often visit each other. With best wishes to you and all Good Company.

Northwest Territories   PEARL

GOOD COMPANY, *Family Herald and Weekly Star*
March 28, 1900

Dear Hostess:

For some time I have been desirous of joining the G.C. Circle. It was four years last November since we left England, and have been a constant reader of the Family Herald and Weekly Star for over two years and enjoy reading it very much, especially the G.C. Circle.

When we left England I thought we were leaving behind the only country I ever should love, but since coming to this country I have changed that opinion, for I have found in this new land a condition which I have never dreamt of, for here in this western country there is a beauty and a vastness which can scarcely be comprehended by those who have not seen it, and the scenery is so different from that in England.

My father settled in a beautiful part of Alberta, where the country is park-like in appearance, and in the summer the trees and flowers are simply lovely, so we like our new home very much. I am at present staying with a married sister in Southern Alberta, who has been the sweetest little girl I ever saw. The place is about one hundred twenty miles from home. Here I have a charming view of the Rocky Mountains, whose hoary heads are often seen far up above the clouds. These mountains are beautiful in winter, looking like sentinels clothed in ermine robes, or the ghosts of King Borea's host mounting guard over Alberta.

Sometimes warm winds come across the Rocky Mountains which are called "Chinooks." During these warm spells it is pleasant to ride or drive, and I wish dear Hostess, you could join me in a run over the prairie, and see the nice fat cattle and horses which run at will here among the foothills of Alberta. Perhaps some other time I may tell you more of doings in Alberta.

With good wishes for yourself and all the G.C. Circle.

ALBERTA FAWN

GOOD COMPANY, *Family Herald and Weekly Star*
August 18, 1900

Dear Hostess:

I have been a reader of your beautiful circle for some little time, and think it is a blessing to a great many of the poor, and I am about to ask you for help also. I am a very poor woman, so poor that the stamp and paper with which I write this letter were given to me by a kind friend. I live with my husband on a farm some miles from town and have most of the work to do, for my husband is almost helpless, having hurt his back some time ago lifting logs. It is hopeless to look for his full recovery for he will always be in the same helpless state as at present. What I ask of you, dear Hostess, is clothing, partly worn of any kind, as we cannot afford to buy any and it is quite cold here just now. I would also like reading matter or old novels of any kind for my husband, as that is about all he can do. I will now close, hoping, dear Hostess that I am not asking too much.

Alberta   EMMA ROSE

GOOD COMPANY, *Family Herald and Weekly Star*
August 18, 1900

Dear Hostess:

May I become a member of your friendly G.C. corner? I have read the
letters for over two years, and I have enjoyed them very much. I live in
the North-West and I love the great prairie, but sometimes tire of it and
long to be in the city. We used to live in a large town before coming out
here. So many of our friends have left for South Africa: nearly all were
in the Mounted Police. My brother has joined the Strathcona Horse. I
do long for this war to be over, as so many homes are desolate with the
loss of loved ones.

I have one of the best of husbands and two little children, the oldest
a girl and the youngest a boy. I saw that English Emma would like maga-
zines. I have a few I can send her if she will send me her post office
address. We live on a detachment a few miles from town, on a river bottom. It is very pretty in summer, as there are so many trees and bushes.
The Old Man's River runs about twenty yards from the door, and the
Porcupine Hills are just a few miles away. Overlooking them are the
mountains, and they look so majestic.

I close, dear hostess, with best wishes.

EAST WIND

*I must have seen East Wind's brother while watching the Strathcona
Horse parade on the day of their visit to Montreal. We were very proud of
the fine "little regiment," as Lord Strathcona calls his gift to the Empire.*

GOOD COMPANY, *Family Herald and Weekly Star*
December 12, 1900

*A letter like the following makes very cheerful reading at this season of
the year when appeals for assistance are so numerous.*

Dear Hostess:

Will you kindly send me two or three addresses of people living in either
Manitoba, Assiniboia, or Alberta, to whom we could send partly worn
clothing or stockings. We have a quantity of such articles which could be
cut down and made over for children. If the people whose addresses

you send are too poor to pay carriage, please let me know, also the number of persons in the families.

I am now very sorry we had not thought of doing this before. It seems an excellent plan. I enclose a letter-card for reply.

Northwest Territories   E.M.T.

E.M.T.'s kind request was acceded to with alacrity. I thank her sincerely for her benevolent intentions, and hope her beneficiaries will duly appreciate her generous offers of help.

GOOD COMPANY, *Family Herald and Weekly Star*
December 12, 1900

Dear Hostess:

I wrote to the G.C. Circle some time ago, but as I was not a subscriber to the Family Herald at the time I suppose I could not be admitted as a member. Since then a kind friend has sent in a subscription for me, so I venture to write again. Seeing in your column week after week how many of your correspondents are so kind and helpful to the needy ones, I hoped perhaps when others worse off and needing help more than I do have their wants supplied some kind friend would take an interest in me and give me a little help. Like very many more in this country, we had a very small crop, and most of that spoiled with the excessive rain. We have no wheat to sell, nor seed for next year, and only enough for our grist and chicken feed. Having six little girls under twelve, I am at a loss to know how to get them some warm clothing for this bitter weather, and should be so thankful if anyone would send me any warm clothing. I am handy with my needle and used to make over-clothes, so should be so glad of anything. My elder girls have each had a good warm coat given them, but I should so like warm hats or hoods: in fact anything will not come amiss. I wish I could apply to that member who so kindly gave her suggestions of making bed quilts for poor ones, for I am much in need of bedding. I would gladly help anyone if I had the means. You cannot think how it hurts me to have to ask strangers for help, but you enter so heartily into the joys and sorrows of your correspondents that I feel sure, if possible, you will mention my case to some of your wealthy members. Christmas is near now, but we shall have no little feast for the poor children, for we have to do without luxuries of all kinds this year. I hope you will forgive me for bothering you with my troubles, but I do not know who to turn to in my distress. I am unable to pay freight on any parcel, but anything sent to my post office address will reach me, as the station joins the office.

Manitoba   LATE COMER

Will not some kind members in Manitoba befriend Late Comer? It would be easy to make a warm hood for a child out of a small remnant of dress material, lined with flannelette. A little petticoat, nightgown, or mittens would not cost much, and a few such gifts from various sources would make an appreciable difference to Late Comer whose address I will gladly send to enquiring members. I will ask Prairie Chicken to put her on the list for a quilt.

———————

GOOD COMPANY, *Family Herald and Weekly Star*
July 31, 1901

Dear Hostess:

Will you please thank Doris for her kindness in sending me some reading matter? I ought to have written before, but I am kept too busy, and the mail only comes once a week. I have also received some Ladies' Journals and nice pictures. I don't know if I have to thank Doris for them too. It is very nice of the G.C.C. to take so much trouble for strangers. I especially appreciate it, as in this part a Scandinavian is looked down on as something inferior. I once heard a remark made by an Englishman that he would as soon shoot a Scandinavian as an Indian. I suppose he thought they both belonged to some other race. I have a nice friend among the English here, but for the most part they would as soon dream of associating with the animals as with us. I don't think they really know how they hurt one's feelings. What a bright lovely world this would be if there was more kind women, dear Hostess. You seem to have a kind word and a helping hand for anybody that comes in your way. God grant you many years to go on with your noble work. I have the hope of one time meeting you to tell you all the help and kindness you have given us in your weekly talks.

Manitoba   SOUR GRAPES

I feel as if I should apologize to Sour Grapes for the rudeness and injustice of those among our countrymen of whom she has cause to complain. I want to assure her that all Canadians of English birth are not so deficient in fine, right feeling. In our Good Company, at least, the same cordial welcome is extended to Scandinavian members as to the English, Irish or Scotch. I hope others as well as Doris will bear out what I say by sending some proof of friendly feeling to Sour Grapes. I shall always be pleased to hear from her.

GOOD COMPANY, *Family Herald and Weekly Star*
March 26, 1902

Dear Hostess:

I have been thinking that some of the readers would be wondering what a cowgirl is. Well, it is a girl who looks after a bunch of cattle on the open prairie. It is a nice job in summer when it does not rain or the mosquitoes are not too bad. If it rains, then the cows turn their backs and go before it, sometimes going miles in a single night between dark and daylight, or until some creek stops them, for they will not cross water in the dark if the banks are the least bit steep. The same with the mosquitoes, only they face the breeze and go right ahead. I usually have to ride between thirty and forty miles a day, often more; it depends on the cattle. In the fall it is easy, as they have to stay around the creeks or springs for water. Then, as I am fond of hunting coyotes, I take out the hounds. I generally get one or two every time I take them out. I just had two dogs this fall and they are both small. I had to help them kill the coyote. I will try to describe a hunt. I always ride along slowly so as not to tire the dogs—just fast enough to keep them behind, for if they see a coyote ever so far away they will always run and you cannot stop them. When I see one I never pay any attention—just go on the same, until I am as close as the coyote will let me. Then I call to the dogs "Coyotey-ote!" two or three times, and start in the direction in which he has gone as fast as the horse can go. Flo, my horse, is very keen on the chase, so she does not need any urging as some others do. We usually have to run about a half a mile, some times more; it depends on the start. Lady, the swiftest dog, stops the coyote till the other one gets up. When Fly got there, she just jumped on top and over and over they rolled, coyote and dogs together. If it was a large one, it would get up again, then the same thing over again, until Lady gets him by the throat. The other crushes his ribs in. The coyote always makes a brave fight for his life, snaps and bites whenever he gets a chance. Sometimes the dogs get pretty badly bitten. They never do if I can help it. If I had not a stick or something along, then off would come one of my long top-boots, which are good and heavy, and down it would come crash on his head. That would stop his biting. One day the dogs killed two and started a third, which was a big one, and they were tired. So first of all, Flo, my horse wanted to jump on top, only I was afraid to let her for fear of the dogs getting hurt. When the dogs downed it at last, I jumped off and kicked it in place of taking off my boot as usual. I tried to jam my foot into its mouth so as to break its lower jaw, as I have often done before. This time the coyote was too quick for me; he caught me clean through the boot and left his teeth marks in my boot—the first time I have been bitten. I pulled off my boot then and went for him in earnest. We soon killed him. In winter I do house work like other girls. I sew and knit, so do not think me any worse than I am.

Cowgirl

Good Company, *Family Herald and Weekly Star*
May 13, 1903

Dear Hostess:

I have long been a silent reader of Good Company, and I enjoy your weekly talks very much. It is a great pleasure to me to sit down and read for an hour or so, but my eyes trouble me so much that I can read but a little at a time.

I, too, am a farmer's wife, and only nineteen. We have a nice, comfortable home, but I feel very lonely at times. Dear Hostess, can you wonder that I feel lonely when I tell you that only a short time ago I lost my two babies, one a little over a year old, and the other an infant. I have never been strong since, and I don't think I ever will be again. It is a trial for me to get my work done. I am going to try to have a little garden this year. I have some cabbage and tomato plants up already. Will some of the members kindly send me slips for house plants, as I like flowers very much and mine got frozen in the winter. I would send reading matter in exchange. Tending plants and flowers will help to pass away many lonely hours.

Wishing you and the Circle every success.

Assiniboia   Maid o' the Mist

Poor little mother! I can share your sorrow and loneliness. I know how the heart is wrung by such a sad loss as yours. I have been very close to those who have suffered in the same way. I earnestly hope the years will bring you bright compensation for these early sorrows.

Good Company, *Family Herald and Weekly Star*
May 20, 1903

Dear Hostess:

Just a line to you and the Circle to thank-you for the kindness I have received. I have had a great deal of trouble and have been sick with the grippe, and have rheumatism in my shoulders so that I can hardly hold a pen. My little girl two and a half years old has been very sick with bronchitis. She has recovered now, but it is so hard for me to tell you the worst. My sweet baby boy, that God gave me on the 16th of December, He has also taken him from me. He died on April 3rd. He had pneumonia, and had almost recovered, but his heart was so weak the doctor was afraid he would succumb, but he did seem so much better the day before he died that I went to bed, I was so done up from nursing him. When I awoke at ten minutes past two, he was dead in my arms. Oh, it is so hard to me! I really thought I would go mad. I could not cry, but I felt the blow worse, I believe, than if I had. I know that he is better off, and our Heavenly Father knows best, so I am content to wait His time, and if I am but true to God, I shall see my darling in a better world that this. I don't know that I ought to write, as I have not been able to renew our subscription yet this year on account of so much sickness and trouble, but I hope to before long.

I have a letter from a member of the Circle who thought I had been ungrateful for not acknowledging her kindness to me. I thought I would ask you to explain to the Circle why I have neglected to write, for I really do not know to whom I owe letters, but if they will write again, I will gladly answer.

A Bereaved Mother—M.E.T.

I feel deeply sorry for M.E.T., and regret that she would have been mis-judged by a correspondent. Some of our members are rather hasty in this respect.

———————

GOOD COMPANY, *Family Herald and Weekly Star*
June 17, 1903

Dear Hostess:

I wrote some time ago, but the letter may have been lost, so will try again. I see Veritas would like some seeds. I have a quantity of pansy seed, all colors, mixed, also poppy seed. I think I will send it to you postpaid, and you can give it to any member who wishes to have it. For the benefit of Perseverance No. 2, I will give my experience in bringing up babies. I am bringing up my fifth and have used the same rules all through, and never had a cross baby. First of all, I never on any account neglect their morning bath, give them plenty of fresh air, let them wear woolen shirts and bands (hand-knitted is best): in fact I keep woolen shirts on all my children the year round, and never have any trouble with bowel complaints. When they are teething and the little mouth is hot, I give a teaspoonful of cold water occasionally. I also dip my hand in cold water and gently smooth it over the little head. I give for a three months old baby one teaspoon of fluid magnesia three time daily, one teaspoonful daily if not fretful. I am always careful about my own diet, avoiding anything sour, such as pickles. I very seldom touch coffee and drink very little tea. Cocoa or milk is much better. I never nurse my baby if I am overheated or excited in any way. I always take a certain amount of outdoor exercise everyday if possible. I do not believe in any kind of soothing syrup. I think if the bowels are properly attended to babies don't need such stuff. I never nurse my baby when I am tired and hungry. I first take refreshment. If any member wishes to know anything that I can tell regarding the care of the dear little lambs, I am willing to write at any time.

Now, dear hostess, I will conclude, but I must add that I enjoy the G.C. page very much, and watch it closely to see if there is any little thing ever so small that I can do to help. I enclose a mite (5 Cents) for the Flannel Fund.

NIL DESPERADUM

GOOD COMPANY, *Family Herald and Weekly Star*
January 20, 1904

Dear Hostess:

I should like to join your Friendly Circle if I may. I read the G.C. letters with great interest. We have taken the Family Herald for a long time and would not like to give it up. We are renewing our subscription for next year, and I send 15 cents for the Flannel Fund. We came from England twenty years ago and settled in Ontario, in the lumbering district. My husband superintended the Sabbath School. His health was very poor. Eight years ago we came to live with our married son on a quarter section of land. This a grand country, for young people with good health. We live about twenty miles from Brandon. The heavy land will yield forty bushels of wheat per acre; the light land about 15. Our wheat was badly damaged by the snowstorm. We have all we need but warm clothing. We are 64 years of age, and we feel the cold. Our minister was in our house last week. He remarked that we had not been out to church for a long time. He looked sorry for us. I think he guessed the reason. We have five miles to go to church. We have the Bible and a few good books, but still, it is very pleasant to meet with our Christian friends.

Wishing the G.C. and yourself, dear Hostess, a very happy and successful year.

Manitoba   FRANK'S MOTHER

If any kind member of our Circle living in Manitoba can spare some warm clothing for Frank's Mother or her husband, I shall be very pleased to send her address on request.

––––––––

GOOD COMPANY, *Family Herald and Weekly Star*
April 12, 1904

Dear Hostess:

While your charming circle was still in its infancy I became a member and received a pin. I have never written since, still I have kept a close eye on its growth and must say we are quite a community now. When I wrote you before I was a girl in the very eastern part of Ontario. Now I am a wife and a mother, and live in one of the charming valleys of British Columbia, two hundred miles from the coast, in the Okanagan district. We have a very mild winter, scarcely any snow. I, like several other members, am a farmer's wife. I have lived in town part of my life, too, and I liked it very well. If I could have my cows and chickens and garden in town I would not mind living there. I have a baby girl two years old. There are no neighbours within a mile of me; my husband is away a great part of the time and I am very lonely. I am very fond of reading, making lace, and cushions and quilts, so time passes all too quickly.

Dear Hostess, how I do enjoy your weekly talks; they seem to cheer me on; you have no idea the amount of good you are doing. I trust you may be long spared to lend us a helping hand, as you have done in the past four years. Now dear Hostess, some poor member in Manitoba or N.W.T. wished for some print pieces for quilts. If you could send me her address I could send her some. I wish I could do more for the Circle, but what papers and books I get I pass them on to a neighbour who gets none.

With best wishes to you and all the charming circle.

British Columbia   BLUEBIRD

P.S.—You may give my address to anyone wishing it. The address asked for was sent to Bluebird, whom I thank sincerely for her kind words and active interest in the Circle. I hope to hear from her again.

——————

GOOD COMPANY, *Family Herald and Weekly Star*
May 4, 1904

Dear Hostess:

I have been reading your good paper, and I am much interested in the page for women. I am one of those unfortunate people who came out to the North-West last year brought out by Mr. Barr, I and my four young sons and one daughter, aged 12. We have been very unfortunate in los-ing my cattle. By not having a knowledge of the country, I lost three horses this year: all our hay was burnt, so I find we have all to begin again.

I have been doing dressmaking and nursing to earn a little to keep things going. I feel very lonely out here. The minister lent me one of your papers, and I am a subscriber now, and I feel great pleasure in read-ing it. I am sending them to England for my other son to read. My husband was ill for five years before he died, and I worked and kept my children (7) by my needle, and saved money to come out here, and now I must begin again.

I should be delighted for some of your many friends to write to me, for I feel very unhappy at times. All my boys and little girl are readers, and we miss our books very much.

Northwest Territories   STILL HOPEFUL

I see by her choice of pen-name that Still Hopeful has the true spirit of a pioneer. I am sorry to hear of her losses, especially as they might, perhaps, have been averted, but it is quite likely that a bountiful season will follow the hard winter and bring her some prosperity.

———

PRIM ROSE AT HOME, *Family Herald and Weekly Star*
January 7, 1905

FROM A DRY CLIMATE

Dear Prim Rose:

I have been a constant reader of the Family Herald for some time. I like the paper very much and always turn to Page 7 first.

I will describe the country we live in. We have a very dry climate, in fact some seasons it is too dry. It is a great cattle-raising country with fine rolling hills of bunch-grass.

We have a telephone through here, but no railway; yet we hope to have one soon.

The country is rich with mineral, but the mines can't be opened to any extent until the railway come.

We are fifty miles from the nearest railway station. If any of the readers would like quilt patterns, crochet lace, doily or knitted lace patterns. I would be pleased to send them.

Nicola, British Columbia   SAGE-BRUSH

PRIM ROSE AT HOME, *Family Herald and Weekly Star*
March 15, 1905

LAND FOR SINGLE WOMEN

The following letter raises a very interesting question and one which I should be glad to have discussed in all its bearings by those who are in a position to throw light on the subject. I have not yet looked into the matter thoroughly enough to give an intelligent opinion, but shall make a point of doing so before long. Meanwhile correspondence on the subject will be welcome.

Dear Prim Rose,

Will you, through your helpful columns, suggest the best means of acquiring land by single women. Could it not be represented to the administrators that the time has come when it is necessary for some provision whereby a woman may acquire a homestead without being a widow. Where is the benefit of opening up the agricultural colleges if a young woman must, after gaining theoretical knowledge of the subject—take up some other calling in order to provide herself with the means to purchase land? Is it not a rather useless concession?

I am informed that in a few cases women have been able to lease Government land in British Columbia in 20 acre lots. At the present time however, there is none to be had. Could you not get up some petition for small holdings for women in Southern B.C. for surely that is the most suitable climate for poultry-raising, fruits and small culture generally.

In the present state of affairs, a settler having a large family of daughters is heavily handicapped. There is small chance of "setting them up" when the time comes with only one-quarter section.

Assiniboia   BUTTER AND EGGS

INGLE NOOK, *The Farmer's Advocate*
April 12, 1905

ROOM FOR A CHANGE

Dame Durden:

As regards the happiness or otherwise of the farmer's wife, I am convinced that very few of them would complain or wish to leave the farm, if they had any thought given to their needs or comfort. There are very few women wholly devoid of sentiment or love of the beautiful. As a rule, these attributes are far from a blessing to a woman who lives on a farm. No doubt, there are some farmers who take a pride and interest in their homes, and make of them a spot of beauty: but indeed they are the exception. How often you hear a hard-working farmer's wife say: "Oh my garden is not much to look at. The men will not bother plowing it, and I am not able to dig it properly." Yet you can see those same men sitting on the fence idle long enough to spade the entire garden twice over. I do not mean to say that men should not relax and take a rest, but I do think that they might spade the garden first.

Marriage, in its most sordid meaning, is at least an even partnership between a man and a woman. How often the wife becomes a nonentity as regards the distribution of the proceeds the unhappy, discontented wives of our country testify. Why, or how a man can claim the title of honesty, and at the same time not only cheat his partner in life of her just share and due interest in the joint concerns of life, but even deny her the satisfaction of a deserved word of praise, is beyond me. How would the same conduct appear in the eyes of the public, if it were acted between man and man? The usurper would be justly called a plain thief. Does it make the action noble or honest because it is only a helpless women whom he is defrauding? Were he to act in the same manner with a woman who was his wife, he would be prosecuted as a villain. You may not say the wife has her "keep." Has not the husband his "keep," and his extras in the way of tobacco and liquor? If the men were only honest enough to make a plain, honest statement as to the course of action they meant to take after partnership was contracted, I am positive not one woman in the full possession of her senses would enter into the net. Do men consider it right or just to never let the wife handle one dollar the year around? Is that their idea of the golden rule, or a joint partnership?

How I wish I could take Dame Durden to see some of my neighbor women. Where there is a hen house or garden fence, the women have

put them up; mud roofs on most of the homes, and rain and mud drop-
ping on the table during mealtime; every morsel in the house frozen to
resemble stone during the winter. Is it any wonder women are not content to live like that? When it rains, mud up to the ankle; the men cannot trouble to scrape it off, so come in loaded with mud and manure,
shuffle their feet well, and leave it for their wives to clean up.

We all like to have our labor duly appreciated. Why does the average husband deny the coveted bit of praise for which his wife hungers?
He gave it in abundance when they were lovers. Why not now? Oh,
how an act of kindness or word of praise would lift the heavy heart. It
would not cost even one cent of the beloved object, his money; yet he is
not honest enough to bestow it. Ask him to plant trees around the
home, and you are cursed for your trouble. Ask for a pump or a closet,
the same result follows. Ask for small fruit, you are told you are insane.
Now, this is a really true picture of by far the greater number of farmers'
homes in some vicinities, and it is the lack of all that constitutes a real
home that makes women detest the farm. It remains in the hands of the
farmer to remedy the evil.

Alberta   B.S.

PRIM ROSE AT HOME, *Family Herald and Weekly Star*
April 26, 1905

TEACHERS WANTED IN B.C.

Dear Prim Rose:

I see some of your subscribers in the East would like to get information
about this western country, particularly British Columbia. I have live in
B.C. for about seven years, and during that time have travelled over a
large portion of it. I shall be more than pleased to supply reliable information to any of your readers. I am in the lumber business myself. There
are good opportunities here for any one who is not afraid of
work—particularly teachers, who receive from $25 to $75 per month
and no trouble to find employment.

Fernie, British Columbia   T. LYNCH

PRIM ROSE AT HOME, *Family Herald and Weekly Star*
April 27, 1905

A SPINSTER WHO KNOWS

Dear Prim Rose,

I am an interested reader of all parts of the Family Herald, but especially so of your department, and as I have been worked up to "writing heat," by the articles sent in by bachelors in reply to "Butter and Eggs," whose sentiments are largely mine, I think I will just give those bachelors a prod with my pen.

I have been in Alberta and Assiniboia, have visited numerous ranches, and know that the alluring picture "Nor-West Bachelor" draws of nine-roomed houses and roasting apples has not many counterparts. For the most part the shacks of the members of the bachelor clan consist of one small room about 10 x 12, which is hall, parlor, library, dining-room, and kitchen combined, built of logs, with unpainted floor, and bunks nailed to the sides for sleeping accommodation. Dreary places where love—at least any I could scrape up—would be sure to fly out the window. I have been there, you see (in the shacks, I mean).

I am one of the spinsters—a real old maid. What I want to say is, that for years I have kept my mother and two sisters—delicate girls who have both died young, one three years ago and one lately. Mother and I are alone. I have tried in every way to get a homestead, being the sole support of the family, but as mother is not a widow, am unable to do so. So we have to move around paying rent, whereas if we could only get land by homesteading we would gladly do the necessary work and build a home. Some one says, "Why not build where you are?" Simply because I teach school and teachers never know when they may receive marching orders.

I did intend writing a harrowing article to let you know there are spinsters who could not be relieved by the bachelor's wise idea, and yet who have to shoulder heavy burdens as bread winners.

Then why, if we wish to remain old maids, may we not do so in peace and be given the same rights and privileges as a single man?

Manitoba   A WRATHY SPINSTER

THE QUIET HOUR, *The Farmer's Advocate*
June 26, 1905

YOUNG WIVES

There are few young wives of our farmers who begin their married life with luxury. Generally, the young husband has just started to make the farm pay after a few years of patient working, clearing the land, and building the little home, making things comfortable for the wife who comes to help him.

It is upon this subject of helpmate, that is the keynote of a happy married life, that one desires to speak. When a girl marries, she must not expect the romance of courtship to continue. She is not loved the less for its departure. She now belongs to her husband, and all that interests him and everything he does for her comfort in the home should be appreciated.

During the first year she has much to learn, hitherto, they have seen each other at their best, each desiring to appear more pleasing. Now, left to themselves, many little flaws in the character of each will show themselves—but no one is perfect. Do not worry a man with little trifles, things that annoy a woman are not always understood by a man. Meet him cheerfully, he will always appreciate your welcome, and his home made bright and pretty will be more to him than a gander away from you.

Learn all you can during your first year about careful management of housekeeping. You will take quite a pride in your attempts at any new dish you serve.

You need not be lonely on a farm; there are so many little duties which fill the day. You can always go on making your home pretty. In the spring, there is your garden and chickens—plenty of time to welcome a friendly caller. Whenever one hears of a housewife feeling lonesome and wanting some friend or relations forever with her, one feels she had few resources. Who can be lonely, when there is a book to read or needlework or be done after the mornings work. Keep up your correspondence, it is a pleasure to hear from friends. Try and take a few papers, and exchange with some neighbors.

Get your husband to make things easy for you in and about the house; shelves and cupboards so that your kitchen may look neat and snug. Many a really good fellow has become careless and indifferent when he found his young wife careless of her personal appearance and the house untidy; no system! no management in her work! Make up your mind from the start to help your husband to succeed in all his undertakings, it can be done. Trials will come, but be brave, and always loving. Love is a mighty weapon, use it at all times for good.

When one thinks of the many mothers who have been the mainstay of the home, of the example they show their children, of the endurance under suffering, and the many trials that mothers of large families must pass through, we can only wish to bring into the early married life the spirit of true comradeship without which no such life is complete.

B.C.

INGLE NOOK, *The Farmer's Advocate*
July 26, 1905

A MAN AMONG THE AMAZONS

Dear Dame Durden,

I suppose I have no business to address my letters to your page, considering that I am not a lady, but belong to the "worser" portion of humanity, and am not blessed with a better half yet. My only excuse is that, although I am a "mere man," still I follow the same calling as the learned matrons who write for the Ingle Nook, being the head cook, bottle-washer, manager and entire family of a small shack in Alberta. So, being in that predicament, I most religiously study the Ingle Nook letters, and, alas, sometimes make the fatal mistake of trying my hand at some of the recipes, which, after being subjected to my own special treatment, resemble paper-weights more than cakes. For this reason I should recommend all fellows starting to keep a pig or two: mine actually seem to thrive, thanks to my experiments.

Dough! that awful stuff! How lovingly it clings to one! How difficult to get a finger clear when a fly happens to settle on your nose!

With what almost supernatural care buttons fly off when there is no one around to fasten them on again!

How dirty the floor looks; and how new and clean the scrubbing brush!

How cold, dreary and miserable the whole place looks when returning home at night!

How grand to have no squalling kids around; no one to worry about you, and when you do happen to feel a little lonely, isn't there the dog to pour one's superfluous affection upon? What would we poor fellows do without a dog?

I would like to wind up with a few hints for beginners:

1. Sew buttons on with a fine wire.
2. Don't fill lamp with oil just before making bread; its taste might be a little curious.
3. Never scrub the floor; it always gets just as dirty again.
4. Boil potatoes in their skins; it saves washing them beforehand.
5. Don't view marriage by the one nagging wife you happen to know; remember the others.

Alberta   J.W.

Your case is truly pitiable, J.W. Truly, you'll have to set out ahunting for a solution to all your difficulties. But wait until our competition is over; then you'll know whether to fix your binocular apparatus on a blooming maid of sixteen, or on a practiced old housekeeper of forty-seven. Your household hints are excellent—under the circumstances. Tried recipes, are they?

PRIM ROSE AT HOME, *Family Herald and Weekly Star*
August 16, 1905

A GOOD PLACE FOR WOMEN

Dear Prim Rose:

I have read your columns with very much interest for the last few weeks, and now ask you to give me a little space that I may express my views in the matter. In regard to the West, I think that it is the only place for any boy or girl who is steady and willing to work. They have better opportunities than they have in the East. But if any persons expect to make a living without working, they had better stay away from here, there are too many of that class in the North-West now. If a man is a hustler he can make from $40 to $50 per month by hiring out, and if one works two or three years at this he will soon be in a position to start farming. The unimproved land out here can be had from $1 to $10 per acre, with ten years to pay for it, so if any person wishes to farm he can homestead

160 acres, buy a 160 acres (or more if he needs it), and would have to pay only about $80 per year, which is not much for 320 acres in all.

Now for girls, I think it would be a great mistake for them to come out here merely for the sake of getting a man. There are no doubt some, if not many, young bachelors out here that need a good and loving wife, yet there are some that do not deserve one. While on the other hand, if a girl intends to work out, this is a very good country for her. Girls' wages run from $20 to $40 per month and board. And a good cook can easily get $45 and even more.

Now if any boy or girl wishes to write to me concerning the West, I shall be only too glad to give any information that I possible can.

Wishing your club success.

A Clerk

Correspondence, *Western Home Monthly*
November 1905

To the Editor,

Sir,

I think that it is high time that women had a voice on the subject of race suicide.

First I would like to mention that I love children, better than Bishop Williams, President Roosevelt, or Mr. Evans, for I love them too well to want them brought into the world helter skelter, whether there was anything for them to eat, drink, or wherewithal for them to be clothed, not mentioning education. I beg to disagree with Bishop Williams that people should marry young whether they had any prospects or not. My opinion is that if a couple see that they cannot bring their children into the world comfortably, they deserve credit if they are unselfish enough to postpone their marriage until they can.

If they do marry young and their reverses come, I say it were better for them to resort to a "process of prevention" until brighter days, rather than have the wife and mother, and husband and father too for that matter, worried to death, trying to keep the wolf from the door.

I am not defending the wealthy who for their own social pleasures forego the pleasure of having children. They give up the far greater joy, of them let us say, "Lord forgive them for they know not what they do."

But, the poor already overburdened women and as a professional nurse I have seen some pitiful households and little children that I would like to forget if I could.

Frequently we hear people say, "If the Lord sends them He will see that they are cared for." What about the starving millions in India, in old London and every large city. Yes, and small city too, starving both body and soul.

Another thing, it is hardly fair that women should invariably have to shoulder the blame for childless homes, for while I admit that the fault is usually theirs, I know of several cases where the wife would give almost anything if the husband would consent to her having children.

One of the above gentlemen suggests as a remedy for race suicide, that we show by our actions that the childless are despised. Then what about those to whom children are denied? Are they to be among the despised, or are they to publish their sterility, throughout the land in order to be exempt?

Perhaps this will bring down the wrath of our good bishop, and the others on my head, but I am simply stating what I think, and as far as I can learn what many other women think.

Thanking you Mr. Editor for space in your valuable paper,
        I am very sincerely yours,

Bella Plains, Assiniboia, September 5, 1905   MOTHER

CORRESPONDENCE, *Western Home Monthly*
November 1905

Editor: Western Home Monthly

Dear Sir:

Being the mother of seven children you will understand that I have not much time to write on any subject. Much has been said about "race suicide" and if you will grant me a little indulgence I will add my small quota to the grist that is being said. I attribute the cause of race suicide to the fault finder. I would advise girls to remain single as they are rather than to marry and bring children into a world so corrupt that it is not a fit place for children to live in. Is it not better to have no children, than to have them brought up under some of our present day so-called Christian Governments where the sons of fond mothers are sent forth to give their lives and make home desolate for the purpose of worldly gain. And the agitators of cruel war should be out in the front ranks of battle to be a target for shot and shell, if this be done there would be less war.

Furthermore, the workingman and the poor laborer are taxed and in most cases unjustly taxed to pay the cost of war.

I say, there should be no children until such time as the mothers who have to suffer and rear them will have a voice in the making of our country's laws. I say, let there be no children until such time as our so called worthy governments discontinue the license and sale of liquor and places of vice.

I would like to say much on the all important subject of race suicide, but time and space will not permit, but as a parting shot I will say that I do not admire a woman who does not love children, and to the faultfinder I will say, let men follow the laws of God and women will not continue the race suicide.

So long as governments of so called Christian countries persist in passing unjust and oppressive laws, which directly and indirectly add to the misery of the thousands of half starved and badly neglected mothers and children just so long will race suicide go on. Now, men have the sole right to make laws. Why not extend the franchise so as to give equal rights to women. If women could use the ballot box to prevent some of the abuses that are now permitted by our present law makers, it would prove in the end a remedy for race suicide.

I remain respectfully etc.

Fernie, British Columbia, September 9, 1905   A MOTHER

PRIM ROSE AT HOME, *Family Herald and Weekly Star*
January 24, 1906

A WESTERN TEACHER'S ADVICE

Dear Prim Rose:

I should like to answer Fortune Seeker through your column. She asks if the difference between the pay in the east and in the west is worth the sacrifice of home and friends. I, in answering for British Columbia, say no.

The new school system came into force on January 1, 1906. By this the government, which formerly paid the whole salary, and all expenses of the school, only pays forty dollars a month. Besides this, the government gives a dollar for every dollar raised by the people up to one hundred dollars. Many of the schools have already lowered the salary in their district. Many formerly paying fifty are only paying forty this year.

The board is from twelve to twenty dollars a month. Railway fare is four cents a mile.

No certificate other than one obtained in B.C. is valid. A teacher coming to the province may secure a temporary certificate, valid only in the school named in the certificate and until the next examination in June.

A girl should not come west unless she has friends here and knows where she can begin teaching. In many of the neighborhoods there are only one or two white families. The rest are half-breeds.

I know of a teacher, first class in the east, who did house work in Vancouver, while waiting for a school, last term. The country is overcrowded with teachers.

I have been teaching for two years since coming to B.C. three years ago, and know something of the teacher's life here.

As I expect to be teaching in a lonely place this year, I should like correspondents in Ontario and the Northwest. Prim Rose has my address.

Wishing the club a happy New Year, I will sign myself,

Vancouver   WESTERN TEACHER

PRIM ROSE AT HOME, *Family Herald and Weekly Star*
March 7, 1906

A WORD FOR WIDOWERS

Dear Prim Rose:

I do not think your readers, who are teachers, feel any surprise at the number of their profession who are enquiring about employment in the West. The chances to marry, happily perhaps, ascinate [*sic*] their weary work-worn brains until it seems they would just marry anyone to escape the horrors of anywhere from 50 to 70 "young barbarians" turned loose on them daily.

But let us teachers have a care. Every year I see numbers of teachers marrying men below their station or who they think can save them from the daily tortures of another term of school, often have to resume work in less than two years to avoid being a dowdy fright in the matter of dress.

I think a teacher who has educated herself to the work can hardly be happy with such narrow, unlightened lives as some of our western farm youths live. If she doesn't marry someone who is very able to give her his intelligent, congenial companionship and good home (and it must be a love affair) she had better remain single and go on teaching and have just one to support.

I think woman's highest calling is wifehood and motherhood, and I think many bachelors are such because they value their personal comforts too much, or are too mercenary to support a wife. Another thing, some teachers want to cast in their lot with some callow conceited youngster that is too overwhelmingly conscious of his own worth for any good use. A woman ages much more rapidly than a man and some of the young things can't appreciate a woman near their own age. It is my opinion that many a teacher would marry far more happily if she married a man a good deal older than herself for he could appreciate her worth and value her as a treasure and she would not need to compare her prematurely aged or rather experienced schoolroom expression with the young chap's youthful beauty and innocence. Moreover, he would probably be able to give her a home along with his love so that her return to teaching might be postponed or even negatived.

I think with a recent correspondent that widowers are a far more manly lot than many of the bachelors, for they have not been too cowardly and selfish to come out and take their places in the world, which is to give love and protection to some women. What if the widowers have got a couple of children! We must be queer teachers if we can't open our arms and our hearts to our loved one's children after having to endure the tortures of some of our half-hundred or more whom we have to comfort, coddle and instruct every day in our professional work, and in spite of parent's grumbling.

Another thing, some women can't stand the work on a farm. If you can't, don't marry a farmer, unless he is able to keep help for you. The small modern house of a professional or business man is far more suited to many teachers than the farm.

Some of my profession may condemn me because I am not enthusiastic about my work. It has good points, of course. At present I am very pleasantly situated. This is the pleasantest school I have taught. All the teachers, except the principal board at the same place, just a few steps

from the school house. Still it has its soul trials. It is better than support-
ing yourself and a man, however, so I say, unless you marry for love, and
a man who is able to support you, stay with it, but stay single.

YOUNG SCHOOLMA'AM

PRIM ROSE AT HOME, *Family Herald and Weekly Star*
March 21, 1906

A HAPPY WESTERN TEACHER

Dear Prim Rose:

I think Wrathy Spinster had been unfortunate in choice of locality. My
experience has been the opposite. I passed third class examinations in
July (I was sixteen), got a permit, applied for a school, put on long
dresses, and did my hair on top of my head, to make myself look old,
and commenced teaching 1st September, ending with the year. I had
2-1/2 miles to go with umbrella, mackintosh and rubbers for rainy
weather, fur coat, storm collar and overshoes for winter. I did not mind
it much, although it was cold kindling the fire, my fingers nipping.
While the threshing gang was in my vicinity, I fared very well, some of
them kindled it for me. I had a good boarding place. Father, mother, a
daughter and two sons. We visited, had visitors, went to dances, socials,
played ping-pong and had a good time. The older school girls said they
would not go to "that kid." I was very proud of my first earnings.

I went to school after Xmas and wrote on second in July, got
another permit, and a school 40 miles from home. This one was similar
to the first, but I took diphtheria. Just think of a little girl of seventeen
sick, not allowed to write, and 40 miles from home, every one scared to
come near you, but I was too sick to mind. The doctor treated me with
antitoxin, and I was able to resume my duties in three weeks. I never
walked home for two months, a gentleman managed to pass at closing
time and took me for a long drive. After Xmas, I went to Normal,
reserving enough of my earnings to pay expenses and in the meantime
applied for another school, fifteen miles from home, commencing
March 20th to end with the year. That was the year of the flood (as we
say in reference to it). I boarded with a cousin, a half mile from school,
but I had to walk too, going around sloughs, jumping streams. I was wet
to the knees, but at recess I kicked a football until I was dry. I was given

a holiday to go to a football match, we had to cross a stream where the bridge was swept away. My cousin and I stood on the plank while Sandy drove through. I was bursting with suppressed laughter at our ludicrous position. The young wife saying, Oh! Sandy dear; and I shouting, Oh! Sandy, your boots! your boots! his running shoes had dropped out and were floating down stream. The roads dried and I wheeled home Friday returning Sunday after dark, afraid of the bogies catching me.

My last school, 15 miles from home, is all up-to-date. I board with a nice old lady, her son and a niece a quarter mile from school. I go skating, dancing and to game parties, visit the homes of my pupils in turn with reading, fancy work, sewing (I make my own clothes) and school duties. I have not time to be melancholy.

The worst encounter I had was when a man pestered me with his attentions (a really nice young man). To avoid meeting him I took refuge behind a sheltering clump of willows, my heart beating like a trip-hammer I thought he would hear. Oh! don't laugh; I was never so scared. He was more bother to me than all the mosquitoes or flies I ever saw.

I wonder if I might suggest an idea. When I was a child I had the misfortune to have a little taken off my thimble finger. If some good genius could invent one to fit me! I have to sew without one. It would have to be made with a hinge and clasp, with the large end down.

Where are Bab and Ichabod's Auntie? I'm afraid those western bachelors are getting too much.

B.A.M.

PRIM ROSE AT HOME, *Family Herald and Weekly Star*
May 16, 1906

ON MINING SPECULATION

Dear Prim Rose,

For a long time I have read with interest the letters of your social corner, and lately I have seen much of love, marriage and money, and quite agree with Mildred Marie, when she states that love goes farther than money.

Although we are in great need of a few hundred dollars in cash, I would not take a million if it was offered me, if it meant that I would have no more of my dear husband's cheerful words of encouragement and ready caresses. We have been married twelve years, but my husband is as much of a lover now as he was before we were married. A house without the true love between husband and wife must be a sad one indeed, even if they have plenty of money; but I must admit that a little money brought into the home where love is so plentiful would make life a bit brighter. I often think over what mistakes we have made and wonder if other married couples are as foolish. The first eight years of our married life my husband had a position in a business house that brought him $75 per month and all our household expenses free, and yet when the company failed and we left the place we had not a cent in the bank. My husband does neither drink nor gamble, and I am not very extravagant, and one would wonder where the money went. I was young, not more than eighteen years when married, and I suppose I used money more freely than I would do now if I had the same chance, and my husband denied me nothing. I was sick a good deal the first years and that cost him a great deal of money; but where we made our mistake was in investing our money in mines. British Columbia has a good many new mining districts that are only in the prospectus state, and young people who are working for a salary have no business to touch those prospects, for ninety-nine times out of a hundred it is a losing game. I said my husband did not gamble; but in mining we did, much to our sorrow in after years; but when the fever catches us we always expect to win and become independent. I was as much to blame as my husband, for he never goes into any undertaking without consulting me first, and if I had objected he would never have done as he did, but it is too late now. The next couple of years put us into debt that now hangs like a load on me always, for it seems we cannot shake it off. Many would smile at the thought of a debt of $500 seeming so terrible to me, but I feel as if I have not the right to the food I eat as long as our debts are not paid. We are striving to get a start on a piece of land in one of British Columbia's valleys, and we have a very small house built which we live in and by careful managing we can live plainly on what my husband makes on odd jobs during the year, but we cannot seem to put anything by for the creditors, but I hope we will manage soon. If that was only off our shoulders we would soon be independent and the happiest couple in the world, I think. What I meant to say was to tell young girls who are situated as I was to profit by my mistake. If you have a kind and indulgent husband, do not buy everything you want, but get what you need and put the surplus in the bank, if is only a dollar a week. It will count up in time, and is safer there than in mines, where you will keep throwing good money after bad, year after year, doing assessment work and paying taxes, trying to hold on, so as not to lose what you have invested, just to find that you have to give up all in the end after all. That kind of speculations are all right for rich people, perhaps, but the ordinary wage-earner must give it a wide berth; the odds are too many against him. If my letter is not too long for publication, dear Prim Rose, I hope some young girl may see it and profit by it.

British Columbia   POOR BUT HOPEFUL

CORRESPONDENCE, *Western Home Monthly*
August 1906

BIG MIKE WANTS A WORKING WIFE

Editor:

I would like to correspond with some of the fair writers in the Western Home Monthly. I am young, temperate, a member of Christ's church, have a half section of land, good horses and cattle. I would like to have a good strong woman for wife who would milk cows and feed calves, and raise plenty of fowl and keep a good garden.

BIG MIKE

HOME LOVING HEARTS, *Free Press Prairie Farmer*
February 6, 1907

Dear Editor and M.B.A. Friends:

That was a capital idea, viz., organizing a mutual help association. It will fill a real want for the women on the prairie. The name is splendid. The Free Press is a weekly visitor. I am so glad you thought of this: let us all help a little to make it a splendid success.

Living, as many of us do, on the bleak prairie, hundreds of miles from civilization, we welcome everything that tends to make our life more bright and cheerful. I came out here when the prairie was but a barren wilderness, and have learned to prize the little things that go so far to make life bearable. A letter from a friend, a piece of poetry, a book or a friendly greeting from a neighbour; these seem trivial things when we are surrounded by friends and plenty; but when we must leave all behind, and go where stern duty bids us, we learn to value little things.

My path has been thorny at times, but still I am thankful for the lessons taught, and some day the reason shall be clear. Friends, let us help one another, and be happier ourselves in so doing. Let us have helpful suggestions and hints on how to make life bright for ourselves and others.

Could we not exchange different articles as well? If anyone cares for it, I could send some hints on home-made furniture.

We live a day's drive from any town, and it is not easy to get everything you would like to have; but it is quite interesting to be out here when you catch the spirit of the prairie. My heart goes out to the woman and children who come out to help build homes on the prairie. If I had the means, I would open a "rest-room" where these people could come in and find a nourishing meal, daintily cooked, a clean warm bed and a bright cheerful fire, thus enabling them to go forth better prepared to take up the struggle again.

This is my ambition. Can some of you, friends, suggest some way in which my plans can be realized? A noble band has come forth to build homes in this glorious west, and the happy homes of our land are our "bulwarks of safety." Let us open wide our doors and keep our fires burning brightly to welcome the "stranger at the gate."

Gathering seed, we must scatter as well: God will watch over the place where it fell. Only the grain of the harvest is ours; Shall we plant thistles or shall we plant flowers?

I have a skirt pattern, 26 inch waist measure and 42 inches long: also waist pattern, 36 bust measure, I would give it to someone who would send postage.

Yours truly,

Saskatchewan   MARIE

Marie has our very best wishes in her noble struggle with the difficulties of pioneer life. Truly, it is a happy life, if one enters into the spirit of it, but not all can do it. I am sure there will be someone who would be glad to get hints from Marie.

M.B.A., *Free Press Prairie Farmer*
February 20, 1907

To the Editor of Home-Loving Hearts:

May I also join the M.B.A. [Mutual Benefit Association]? My credentials are, twenty-one years spent on a farm in this western country, far from post office, store or doctor. Like all other pioneer women, I have in that time acquired quite a little store of practical knowledge, most of it from that hard, but excellent teacher, experience. If this knowledge, embracing, as it does, cookery, curing of meats, dairying (home-made cheese-making a speciality) gardening and sewing of all kinds, can be of any use to others, I will be more than glad.

Also I wish to say that if there happens to be among your readers any girls who have been left motherless, with a number of young brothers and sisters to care for, they are the ones I would particularly like to help. Having been through the mill myself, I am in a position to thoroughly understand the many difficulties of the little woman so placed, and think I could in more ways than one be a help to them and help brighten their lives.

Can our editor or any of the members tell me if there is such a thing as a woman's exchange in Winnipeg? And if so, what are the rules by which it is governed? I have a rather happy knack of making hand-painted and embroidered articles, suitable for Christmas and birthday gifts, and would like to make a little pin-money that way if possible.

MEADOW RUE

No, there is not a "Woman's Exchange" in Winnipeg. The matter has been discussed, and many realize the need for such an institution, but nothing definite has been done as yet. L.L.

Plate 1. Homesteaders Sebina Jacobson and Johanna Solberg, Berry Creek, Alberta, circa 1912. Jacobson is listed in the General Index—Dominion Lands Registry as the registered owner of a half section of land, and Solberg is described in a history of the Youngstown area of Alberta as one member of a three-way partnership that included her husband and her sister Sarah (Glenbow Archives, Calgary, Alberta [NA-206-27]).

Plate 2. Joe Wacha and his wife plastering the walls of their log house, four miles north of Vita, Manitoba, 1916 (W. J. Sisler Coll. 118, Provincial Archives of Manitoba [N 9631]).

Plate 3. A quilting bee, 1902 (Clearview Coll. 1, Provincial Archives of Manitoba [N 12162]).

Plate 4. Alberta woman riding horseback, circa 1910 (Delta Museum and Archives, Delta, British Columbia [1987-23-140]).

Plate 5. Feeding the turkeys, F. W. Crossley farm, Grandview, Manitoba, 1916 (Jessop Coll. 98, Provincial Archives of Manitoba [N 3146]).

Plate 6. Baking bread in a clay oven on the Stefan Scemenczak farm, Fraserwood, Manitoba, 1916 (W. J. Sisler Coll. 101, Provincial Archives of Manitoba [N 9601]).

PRIM ROSE AT HOME, *Family Herald and Weekly Star*
April 17, 1907

TEACHING IN THE WEST

Dear Prim Rose:

Here comes another school teacher from Manitoba and Saskatchewan.

I was seventeen when I first left home, and went bravely off, some two hundred and fifty miles to my first school, and now, six years later, I wish to say in favor of the Western people, that in every place I have been, I have met with great kindness and consideration, and always managed to have a thoroughly good time. I think it is often a teacher's own fault if the people are not nice to her.

I wonder how many of my fellow teachers have experienced the awful loneliness that came over me one spring day when I stood, a forlorn creature, beside my boxes at a wayside flag station and watched the train (my last friend) rapidly diminishing in the distance. There was one other passenger besides myself, whom I envied as I saw him meet his friends and drive off, but no one came for poor me.

Finally when the feeling of desolation was becoming very strong, I saw a great lumber waggon, with a double box and spring seat on it approaching. The big farm horses were plunging through water and half-melted April snow, urged onward by a red-whiskered little man perched aloft on the aforesaid spring seat. It was a mercy I was prepared for emergencies, or else when he drew up beside me, and invited me to ascend I might have looked rather aghast.

"This," I thought, "is rural life with a vengeance," as we went bumpety, bumpety, bump! over the hard icy roads. Since then I have ridden many times in a lumber waggon, often minus even a spring seat. (One of the best times I ever had was a ride ten miles to a picnic, with a merry party of young people, and on that occasion all the "spring" we got was from a straight, smooth board.)

How well I remember the first dinner I had in the district, bacon, fried eggs, and mashed potatoes! How I enjoyed it! And then after the dinner, the drive to my boarding place. The people were away except the three young children who were "keeping house" till papa and mamma came home from town. I sat down, not very cheerfully, I must confess, beside the kitchen stove, on which a big pot of horse feed was boiling. Then I began to conjure up an idea of what my landlady would be like. I had just decided she would be about 45, a big coarse, red-faced untidy Irish woman, with a tongue a long as your arm, when the oldest boy cried out, "Here they come!" The sound of wheel was heard, and the next moment came the freshest, sweetest young matron of twenty-five or thereabouts, you ever saw. She was Irish, with the most beautiful complexion, and eyes and hair, but above all, she had that purely Irish friendliness, so good to a homesick girl. I can't help remarking, before I pass on, what a bright, cheery light that little woman shed through that home and she is only one of the many admirable and noble country women I have met.

The next day was Sunday, and upon my asking about church, I was told service was held in the school house. Methodist one Sunday and Baptist the next. I thought I would much rather stay at home, but of course, that wouldn't do. Some who have passed through the same experience, can imagine the ordeal of that first Sunday, far worse that the first school day. Every one seemed, by the amount of gazing (I will not say staring) directed towards me, to be intensely interested in the new "schoolmarm." It made me feel rather uncomfortable, and I thought, "What dreadful people!" but before the summer was over, I learned to know and understand them better. Some of those same people are my fast friends to this day.

Then followed the first week of teaching. I remember how I calculated each day, what fraction of the whole term I had put in. Every day also meant long walks to the post office so many times to be met with disappointment: I was consumed with homesickness, and I recollect now how longingly I used to gaze after the train as it whizzed past my little school every morning.

The second week brought the first home letter. After that everything seemed all right. Every day I grew more interested in my work, and in the people. In the autumn it was with real regret that I said good-bye to my many friends.

Since then, I have had various experiences, some pleasant, some otherwise, I have walked two miles to school in the winter over unbroken road, have waded through water so deep as to come in over the tops of my long rubber boots, have had salmon sandwiches for two weeks straight for my school luncheon, have wrestled mightily with the dreadful insect, have had to light my own fires occasionally when the thermometer registered 40 deg. below and last, but not least, have had the misfortune to be almost plagued to death by some of the Western bachelors!

But if I walked two miles in the winter, I have also had the pleasure of the early walk in the summer, with the dew sparkling on the grass and wild roses shedding perfume on every side; I have known what it is to have a long, delightful gallop over the prairie; have spend merry Saturdays nutting and berrypicking; have had delicious strawberries and ice cream instead of salmon. Also I have met some bachelors who were not plagues.

Wishing all other teachers and readers of the Prim Rose column, all sorts of luck, and hoping to hear from a few.

Manitoba   IMOGEN

HOME LOVING HEARTS, *Free Press Prairie Farmer*
June 5, 1907

DESIRES TO HELP

Dear Home Loving Hearts:

As the Americans are always very ready to butt in, they do sometimes get butted out for not having license to butt in, having just recently noticed the M.B.A. page, I thought I would try to help Naidanac to see the bright side of our lonely lot. I, too, am living in western Canada, grand old country, with its beautiful landscapes, reaching as far as the eye can see. It is indeed sometimes lonely, but I have had a great deal of experience in being alone. I have learned to forget myself and think more of others, those who really need help, and if we do that we will find someone every day that we can do some little kindness for. No matter how dark our path seems, there is always someone else who has it even darker. I used to feel as Naidanac does. I was quite innocent of Canadian independence and dignity when I came here, but you don't usually have to knock a Yankee, as we are called, down to make them take a hint. Here is one I got a few months ago: I had been home for Christmas and was returning again, having boarded the train at Regina, and was waiting to start. As the engine had to be repaired, we were left on the track for several hours. There were two ladies just opposite my seat. Having to sit and wait so long, time began to hang heavy, so I spoke to one of them, thinking I would get rid of the time, but my remark was resented so quickly, I did not speak any more, but just sat quietly and let others do the talking. I found out that they too, had been home for holidays. They were from Ontario, as I soon found out, by their conversation. I understood at once why I was not wanted to take part in the discourse. I was an American, and they knew it. I was not as clever as they were. I could not tell that they were Canadians. I am rather stupid in that line, I cannot tell an American from a Canadian, although some seem to know one from the other at once. They all look alike to me. She did not seem satisfied with cutting me short, but she managed to get behind me and make fun of me. Oh, I can see her yet; but I feel thankful to-day, that through it all, I did not give her an unkind word. I also found out that she went to church every Sabbath and had the sacred duty of mothering children. I thought, how sad to see a mother raising dear little children in such a spirit as that. I am not a mother. God has not blessed our home with children, but if I should be one, I shall try to teach them the true spirit of humility. How different would be our grand old world if all parents would teach their children to love God and serve Him. Then we would not have time to think of nations as nationalities, for are we not all God's people and is not what we own His? Oh, blind that we are, walking in the darkness rather than the light. Now, I do not wish anyone to think that I am giving all Canadians a hearty breeze, for some of my very best friends are Canadians. There are exceptions everywhere. I am not looking for sympathy, for as long as we do, so much harder will be our burden, for we will have to carry disappointment which is a thing not easily borne. Sometimes I have a blessed refuge where I go and breathe out my woes. On Christ the solid rock I stand. I have learned to say with Jesus, never alone. God is always with me, and will be with anyone who wants Him: and above all, let us be loyal and love God. Beautiful Canada, we can do that and yet love our mother country as the place of our birth. Now let me say to all who chance to read this epistle, if the coat don't fit, don't put it on. I would be pleased to hear from any of the sisters. I would answer any letters from anyone and would be pleased to help some one in any way that I can.

HAZEL EYES

Home Loving Hearts, *Free Press Prairie Farmer*
July 17, 1907

A Brave Woman

Dear Editor—

Have you room in your corner for still another "Homesteader." I have read the letters ever since they began and have at last plucked up courage to write also. I can fully sympathize with the others, who like myself, have left home and friends to come to a lonely homestead in the west. I wonder if there are any others situated just as we are? We are the only Canadians in a settlement of German Americans, some of whom cannot talk English enough to make themselves understood. There are others who talk a sort of "Pidgin English." Sometimes I wonder if I would be able to talk Canadian properly now, I have become so accustomed to making signs, shrugging my shoulders and using the simplest words in order to make people understand. We have been here since last October and only three women have been in our house yet. Our neighbor, the nearest one, is a very nice woman and is learning English very rapidly. Now with one exception these neighbors are not companionable, we had nothing in common, different nationality, different religion, everything different that goes to make life socially speaking pleasant for us. There is no school yet, though lately an application has been sent to Regina for one in this district, and in the meantime we give our little boys lessons everyday trying to do what we can towards educating them.

In spite of all the drawbacks, we like our new home. The green grass, trees and many wild flowers all make a lovely country. The flowers are beautiful, so many different varieties. Each day the children bring in a large bouquet. I wish I could send one down to your office on dusty Portage avenue.

We came from Winnipeg and we miss everything so much though none of us will say we would like to go back to the city to live. We like the free, healthy, happy life out here with no rent to pay, no grocer's bills, no water rates, no street car fares, no butcher's bills and the thousand and one ways of spending money in the city.

If only we had a church and school near us and some English speaking people, and oh! I had better stop. We try to make the best of things as they are and some day perhaps more Canadians will settle near us or if not, we may go to them. I enclose two recipes, asked for and one of oatmeal cookies, all tried and often used.

If I take up so much of your time and space you will not want me to come again.

Wild Rose

P.S. The roses are blooming now.

———

Prim Rose at Home, *Family Herald and Weekly Star*
August 21, 1907

Diana of the Pacific

Dear Prim Rose:

I have been a reader of your paper for years.

I am a western girl living on the shore of the great Pacific Ocean in B.C. I have lived in the west for a number of years, far away from what is commonly termed the civilized world, but to me it seems almost perfect. It is true we have no public schools or churches within miles of where we live, but that fact has no tendency to make our small settlement uncivilized. The roughs of the world are never welcomed to our port. Yet we hope to have a thriving town here some day. No doubt many would ask how I enjoy myself here—to which I will answer, in the first place, I have my parents, also brothers and sisters, nieces and nephews all around me. When the weather is fine we can go for a boat ride and with the fish leaping all about, there is no pleasure more exciting than to draw a beautiful salmon into the boat.

At other times, I take my gun and little dog and go for a hunt into the dark woods, parting my way through tall ferns with the softest imaginable mossy carpet under my feet—slip-slip-slip, ever looking to see what I can find or hear, lest there might be an unsuspecting deer to slay, or a couple of cougars watching for a chance to spring upon me in turn. Although more often than otherwise, I find nothing more than a grouse or a saucy squirrel to carry home with me. At other times I go on the beach at low tide to gather shells and in the evenings we have music. I wish to object to a part of Will. D's letter of June 19th. He says we western girls may talk all day and yet never say anything of interest. Now, I hope I may not be so unjust to him, for indeed he writes an interesting letter, but he reminded me of a hermit crab, and is so pleased with himself and his bachelor accomplishments that he can not do us girls justice.

I would correspond with a middle-aged bachelor or widower who could and would gladly produce a sworn statement by a J.P. that he is perfectly respectable in every way and does not drink or use any profane language. My address is with Prim Rose.

SUNSET

M.B.A., *Free Press Prairie Farmer*
October 23, 1907

FOND OF HORSES AND HUNTING

Dear Editor:

Would I be welcome? I have thought of writing for a long time, and every time my courage would fail, but I made up my mind to stay with it this time. Oh, "Hazel Eyes," I am nearly wild over horses. I can both ride and drive, and nothing suits my taste better than hunting. I wish "Hazel Eyes" could drop in on me and have a week at the prairie chickens, ducks and rabbits. We could bag a few, I am thinking. I would like a pin, but do not understand what the M.B.A. stands for.

BESS

HOME LOVING HEARTS, *Free Press Prairie Farmer*
January 1, 1908

HELPFUL AND AMUSING

Dear Editor and Members.

Just thought I would ask to be allowed to join your friendly circle. I am always an interested reader of the M.B.A. "Maderia Vine," asks if any members live in Saskatchewan. I do, having come here last June, and have found out some of the ups and downs in homesteading, or rather in being the other half of the homesteader. Our crop like "M.V.s" was frozen, but we are not discouraged on that account, my greatest worry at present being the lack of school, three of my children being out of school ever since we came, but we are living in hope of having one in

65

the spring. One member lately asked if any of the members could drive themselves. Now, I would like to ask, can any of them drive oxen? One day lately, my husband being absent with the horses, my little son was left to plow. He came to me after a time feeling unwell. I offered to plow for a while. He came and showed me how to manage the sulky plow, but the only sulky thing about the affair was the oxen. One old fellow was quite willing to go, and the other one was quite willing to let him, provided he could stay behind with me. After an hour's hard work with whip and voice, I was overjoyed to see my boy come and take my place. I have admired his patience ever since. It is so near Christmas. May I wish our editor and members a merry Christmas and a happy New Year. Never in our home has there been so little preparation, for if we had the means, it is impossible to get the usual Christmas cheer, nearer than forty miles. But I have much to be thankful for, I have a husband and five children, all at home in the best of health. I have carefully explained to the children that this country's Santa Claus was frozen out of business this year, so that it will lessen their disappointment at finding their stockings empty this year, for the first time in their short lives. You members living in old and settled parts know little of the misery and poverty of some of these newer and less fortunate sections of the province, with their crops—in most cases the first—all frozen. No work for the men unless going a long distance from home, and in most cases they have no money to take them there. But I have never met a discouraged person; all seem to look forward to something better next year. To all intending coming west, I should say, if it is possible, they should always bring at least one cow and poultry, more if possible, for there is a good market for them or their product; and besides it amounts to a luxury if a family has to buy butter or eggs here. I have met some who brought with them organs and fine furniture and no cow, with the result that, there being no room in their small shack, organ and furniture stood out in all weather and were spoiled, whilst the family bought, when they could, milk and butter. I have already overstayed my time, and will close with best wishes to all. I would like a pin, but Hubby says I'll have to wait until the hens lay to get the price.

BARRIE

HOME LOVING HEARTS, *Free Press Prairie Farmer*
May 20, 1908

LIFE AND LOVE

Dear Members of the M.B.A.

I am so happy this morning. Wonder if telling you all the things that combine to make my sunshine would cheer any other person. We are homesteading. Have a nice piece of land, neighbors galore, and such nice people to make into friends. There are so many nationalities and different religious sects represented, yet to see us gathered together, whether in church, picnics, parties, or simply spending the social evening, you would imagine us a large family. Differences of opinion are thrown to the winds so far as individuals are concerned. Maybe there are a few kickers, but I think they are loved for love's sake. One hears of some misunderstanding, then maybe you'll meet the same party and he will say, "I've got So-and-so's sleigh borrowed"—or "fanning mill," or something. The little ripples do not effect the deep of true neighborly feeling. We are just 2-1/2 miles from one of the new towns of the G.T.P. [Grand Trunk Pacific]. Isn't that just lovely. If you haven't lost part of the cuticle off your back jolting over 50 or 60 miles of prairie trail, you maybe wouldn't know how to appreciate that item of the happiness list. I was so enthused over the novelty of the trail though, that I walked and ran a good many of the long miles my first trip, gathering flowers, exploring sloughs, etc. I am sorry for the people who lost their grain last year. But, oh, the new season is nowhere, with all its plans and possibilities, so we'll "nis [sic] not care," will we? Last year I canned 16 quarts of wild strawberries, besides having all we could eat every night for tea as long as they lasted. Then we went raspberrying, and beside what we ate I canned six quarts of them. After the raspberries came the cranberries. I have a pony and am able to do lots of riding around; also a dog, guitar, chickens; expect to have a garden and flowers, and last but not least, is my house, and an almost perfect husband. I have a rifle, too, and hunt some, but am not a very good shot. Will be able to scare hawks, though, I guess. I'm going to send you my favorite recipe for chocolate cake. We have our homestead named. I wonder if others have named theirs, too. It's quite a fad in our neighborhood. Wouldn't do to tell the names, would it? Be like the little boy who said, "The first two letters of my name are Jim Brown," wouldn't it? Must say good morning for this time.

CRICKET OF PARADISE VALLEY

Cricket—Not much danger of me throwing this away. Your happiness is contagious. We are glad you came. L.L.

———————

CORRESPONDENCE, *Western Home Monthly*
September 1908

A CHANCE FOR A BACHELOR

A lady reader of the Western Home Monthly writes from Calgary to say that there are a number of women in the West awaiting the opportunity to join in a life partnership with the sturdy young farmer or rancher. The letter speaks for itself.

To the editor of *The Western Home Monthly*:

Dear Sir:

In reply to a letter in your last issue re: the marriageable Man. I should like to ask him of what use it would be to send marriageable women from the East to the West when there are so many of them here already. It would be well for the marriageable men of the West to turn their eyes to the marriageable women of the West instead of those away East. I am also in a position to state that there are quite a number of women in the West who are anxiously waiting for such an opportunity as your correspondent speaks of, the saving of a man from a life of dissipation and uselessness.

A MARRIAGEABLE WOMAN

———————

HOME LOVING HEARTS, *Free Press Prairie Farmer*
December 25, 1908

A SAD STORY

Dear Editor:

I have been reading your page with interest, especially the parts interested in the women's dower question. It always seems to me that a bad man can always get the property away from his wife no matter what the law of a civilized government is. Let me tell you my experience in a country where the law was supposed to protect the wife. I married at the age of 18 a man I loved more than my very life, and who professed to love me. I lived with him very happily. Two children were born to us and before the birth of the third one we decided I should go home for a visit and stay with my parents until after the birth of my child. At first my husband answered my letters very regularly, but finally they were neglected for some time. I only received occasional replies. I laid no blame on him as he was a lumber contractor and very busy most of the time, but when the letters ceased entirely I became anxious. I wrote on an average of three letters weekly. Finally my sickness came about and imagine my surprise when I found myself the mother of a pair of twins. I wrote my husband begging him to come and take me home or send money for me to go to him. No answer came to my pleading, but as soon as I could get money to pay my fare, I went to him. Our home was three miles from town. I hired a rig and went to what should have been my home. I arrived there at 10:30 o'clock p.m. amid a downpour of rain. The house was in darkness. We rapped at the door. My heart leaped into my mouth when I heard the well-known voice of my husband in response to our call. When he saw who it was he nearly fainted away. He did not let me in the house, left me standing outside while he went in to talk with some one evidently in possession of the house. He returned in a short time and told me he did not consider me his wife any more and to get off his place. I begged to know the cause but it remained for the neighbors to tell me. He had taken up with a woman only six weeks after I went home and he took her to his home and lived with her as his wife during my absence. Now for the dower question. He was considered rich in this world's goods. He has not given me one cent from the time I went home and at the time I am writing of I had 35 cents and owed the liveryman $1.00. I had no means to go to law and four little ones to care for. After days of abuse and torture during which a kind neighbour took me in, I was forced to consent to take $75 to pay my fare away out of the country for I would not live where the shame of the father should ever reach the children. Before going I gave him a divorce and the last words I said to him were: "Now, Jack, to-morrow you make arrangements to marry that woman. For my sake don't live in shame and disgrace any longer, and as I forgive you, may God forgive you also." I came here, I went to work and have harbored no ill will. I have worked at anything I could get to support my little ones and last summer my health broke down and I am not in very good shape for winter. I thought perhaps some of your kind members would be willing to help me with some clothing if they have any cast off clothing suitable for a boy of 5 to 9 years old or for myself. I wear 26 inch bust measure and 24 inch waist. I would be glad to make them over into big or small. I would pay postage on them

BREAD WINNER

P.S.—I would like to add that I have entirely recovered from my great grief and am quite content to work to support my family until they can help themselves. So please do not think I am trying to burden you all with a great long tale of woe. B.W.

Bread Winner—I do not know the laws in the United States, but I think you can yet force the father of your children to support them and I think you should do so. It would only be just to you and the children. See a lawyer about it. L.L.

PRIM ROSE AT HOME, *Family Herald and Weekly Star*
February 5, 1909

AN ENGLISHWOMAN'S VIEW

Dear Prim Rose,

The letters of some of your correspondents are amusing. "Verdant Green," for instance displays the very fault for which most Englishmen are disliked by Canadians: he comes over here and talks about the superior knowledge and attainment of Englishmen, etc., as compared with Canadians. I am an English woman; have lived in Canada some fourteen years, and I certainly do not wonder at Canadians being thoroughly sick of hearing about the Old Country and its perfections. If anybody from Canada went over to England and made a similar nuisance of themselves there they would be promptly told to shut up and sit down. For, if there is one thing that English people have learned to perfection, it is the art of keeping people in their proper places, and it is an art Canada would do well to study, for I have noticed that Canadians have far too much tendency to be "hail fellow, well met," with every one they meet. Class distinctions may be an abomination, but they are certainly a convenience in keeping undesirable folks at a distance; for instance, such boors as the one with whom "An Autumn Idyll" is so justly indignant. His place was undoubtedly the kitchen, and in my house he would most certainly have been relegated there, whether he liked it or not. If this correspondent will take a word of advice from me, she will have a good long oilcloth covered table in the kitchen and give the men their meals there; keeping her own private rooms for the exclusive use of her own family. This custom is almost universal out here in the west, on the larger farms, the men all eat in the kitchen, and the mistress of the house and her children have the dining room to themselves. If the men do not like it, nobody troubles themselves much, why should they? If a man thinks himself entitled at all the refinements of life, let him get them for himself as those he works for have done, and not expect to have them given to him gratis. As to one man being as good as another, that is all nonsense. It is this doctrine, par excellence, that is responsible for the discomforts to which Canadians voluntarily submit themselves in associating with people in every way beneath them, merely because they happen to employ them. If "An Autumn Idyll" ever comes across another disgusting boor, she should ask him where he was brought up. It will probably have been in the purlieus [sic] of Drury Lane, or in the neighborhood of Wapping, Limehouse, or Shoreditch, some of the worst quarters of Old London, for I am sorry to say that the greatest hoodlums come from London, and nice specimens of the unwashed they are too. I know that many of the men who work on the farms are nice, well-behaved fellows, but when there is large number of men, at threshing and harvest, for instance, it is, of course, quite impossible to discriminate, and all must be treated alike. Don't give them white table cloths and your best china and glass, a good white oil cloth is a great labour saver, and so are gray flannelette sheets, for workingmen's beds cannot be kept clean unless the men wear pyjamas and they seldom do this.

With best wishes for continued success.

Edwin, Manitoba   TERESA

MAILBAG, *Grain Growers' Guide*
February 1909

THE WIFE'S DOWER

To the Editor of the Guide,

Dear Sir.—In your mail-bag I see a letter from "A Saskatchewan Farmer" concerning the Dower Law and advising the men to sign petitions against it. Now, any one who had been reading the Women's page in the weekly Free Press, the paper to which he refers, knows well enough that he is "off." The Dower Law does not give a wife any control of her husband's property until after his death, when we want the law fixed so that he cannot will it all away from her or mortgage or sell his real estate without her consent. Also the law would apply to every man owning real estate, not farmers alone. There are lots of cases where men leave their wives and run away with other women leaving their wives destitute. As he has married her and so prevented her from earning her own living, as there are generally little ones to support, it is only fair that she should have the right to some of his property and also some say as to whether her home is sold or not. Now who should a man leave his property to, if not his wife? This law will not affect good husbands as they will leave it to their wives anyway and those who do not intend to, should be made to. You know the saying "A bird that can sing and won't sing should be made to sing." At any rate we hope and believe that the appeal to sign against it will fall on deaf ears as we know lots of the men would not be as selfish as A Saskatchewan Farmer.

Let me whisper something to you. This same man wrote to the Woman's Page of the Free Press, which allows men's letters while the Dower is discussed, and signed himself "Justice Equal." He says since this came up "my wife has heated discussions with me." Did you ever know of a heated discussion in which only one took part? He also says he has been unable to work for five years. Don't you think his wife deserves all his property if he has spent all his time in the house? I do pity that poor woman. However we trust that such men are rare and we believe that few if any will answer his base appeal. And another thing, he has been told so often through the Free Press, the opinion the women have of him that I guess he is feeling rather sore. Ah "Justice Equal" I recognized you right straight.

As to springing it on you all of a sudden, that is folly as we want everyone to know the way the law now stands, that a man can sell everything and leave his wife and children penniless, as we expect the men will rectify it, once their attention is drawn to the subject. Is it fair that a woman work all her life and then perhaps be left without a cent of what she has helped to earn? Methinks I hear the echo of the shout from many throats No! No! No!!!

Help us you Grain Growers for the sake of your own daughters.

I will sign my Free Press pen-name.

Manitoba, February 1, 1909   LORD ULLIN'S DAUGHTER

MAILBAG, *Grain Growers' Guide*
March 1909

THE DOWER QUESTION

To the Editor of The Guide:

If you will kindly allow me space in your paper to try and correct Lord Ullin's Daughter on the dower law I will be greatly obliged. She referred to the dower law as not giving the woman any control over her husband's property until after his death. Now, if I have any brains I take it that if the dower law was in force the man could not either mortgage the farm nor sell it without his wife's consent, and I consider that gives the woman power that she is not entitled to.

They cannot force a woman to pay a man's debts while they are living together, and when he is dead the creditors will look after their pay. Lord Ullin's Daughter claims there are lots of cases where a man runs away from his wife with other women. If those men are farmers who run away from their wives, who does the work on the land?

Are women who are doing the kicking also doing the work? I don't think so. Those are the women who are dissatisfied and maybe would like to run away with another man, only they would like to take their husband's money along with them. Now if their husband runs away with another woman the law compels the man to support his wife, but if the woman runs away with another man what redress does the man have? None. Now I wish to know if Lord Ullin's Daughter considers that a square deal. She claims that the man who doesn't intend to leave his property to his wife should be made to. I take it that all women are good wives and worthy of the property. But I am prepared to tell Lord Ullin's Daughter that some women are not fit to carry the name of woman, much less a man's money; But I do not put them all under this class. I am not selfish, however.

If a man happens to die first, let his wife have the benefit of the money while she remains a respectable widow, and then at her death let the money go to the family, not to some other man who might marry the widow.

Now, Mr. Editor, I think you were wise in publishing Lord Ullin's Daughter's letter without passing your opinion on it, and have no doubt you will accord me the same privilege. Thanking for your anticipation,

I remain,

MERE MAN

———

HOME LOVING HEARTS, *Family Herald Weekly Star*
July 14, 1909

PRETTY AND USEFUL SEAT

Dear Miss Laurie and Members:

It is a long time since I wrote before and I have been receiving so much benefit from the letters written by others, I thought I had better send a little information myself and hope it will help some one. If it is not too late it may benefit Pansy Blossom a little anyway. I papered our shack, which is 16 × 20, with building paper, ceilings and sides. I say ceilings as I have two rooms, although they are small, I had just rough lumber to work on, but the building paper goes beautifully, and with a little patience you can get it on as smooth as glass. I made my paste out of flour just the same as for wall paper, only much thinner, as the building paper is much harder to wet than the other. I cooked the paste on the stove for a few minutes after adding the boiling water, and as it cooled and got thicker I added more water and kept it thin enough to wet the paper well, but not right through. I also pasted the wall before I put on each piece, and lapped the edge just a trifle and pasted it also. The paste does not mark the building paper, so one does not need to be particular in pasting it, only to get it on smoothly and be sure each piece is well patted down and stuck before you leave it. It takes some hours for it to dry, but as long as you are sure you have it all pressed firmly to the wall you are all right. I then did mine all over with wall paper. I got a small pattern with stripe effect for the walls, which makes the rooms look larger. I built a corner seat extending from the corner about four feet along each wall and a good foot wide, with a removable top, and as high as an ordinary seat. I use it to hold all my bed linen and have the one end for to hold my sewing and mending. I made a long cushion and a short one just like a mattress to fit the top and painted the rest blue to match. I dyed some canvas bags I had to match the blue and I put it around the wall at the back about 2-1/2 feet from the seat up and finished the top with a Greek key design worked in silk about four inches from the edge. The blue canvas looks like burlap and no one knows the difference and I have a pretty corner as well as a useful one and it only cost me a few cents. We are enjoying the beautiful days now. The mosquitoes are not so plentiful as other years. I keep them out pretty well, as I have screens on everything they can be put on. I saw the letter from "A Young Wife," last week and I thought if she would write me I might be able to help her a little, but not if she meant infants' clothes. I have a few little things left but not any smaller. She could have them if she would write me. I do not want to sell them, so she need not fear one. I can at any time. Would you kindly forward the enclosed letter to "Gweno." I must not take up any more of your time, so will close by wishing all a successful season.

BRIGHTNESS

Brightness—I was most interested in your description of the way you fixed your house. I am sure it must be fine and I know your suggestions will help many others. It is such helpful hints we like to get—L.L.

PRIM ROSE AT HOME, *Family Herald and Weekly Star*
August 18, 1909

THE DOWER LAW

Dear Prim Rose,

In 1882 the Manitoba Legislature passed an act abolishing the dower law which gave the wife one-third interest in landed property. This was done in the boom time to facilitate the deeding of land without sending papers to Ontario and back for the wife's signature as most of the men had wives in the East at that time. The dower law has not been called for since then in this province, husbands and wives alike being satisfied.

At least as much property is held here by wives as in Ontario, in proportion to numbers. Wives in Manitoba get better treatment from their husbands than they would get from the law. Only the Ontario women get excited about the oppression of Manitoba wives by their husbands.

JUSTICE OF THE PEACE

HOME LOVING HEARTS, *Free Press Prairie Farmer*
September 22, 1909

BABY FOR ADOPTION

Dear Miss Laurie,

A friend of mine has a dear baby girl, which she would like to get adopted. Now, dear Miss Laurie. do you know of anyone who would like to adopt a baby of three months? She is using the bottle and is quite healthy.—Mrs. J.A.K.

Mrs. J.A.K.,—I am sure many will want the wee baby.—L.L.

HOME LOVING HEARTS, *Free Press Prairie Farmer*
December 9, 1909

A STRONG PLEA FOR WOMEN

Dear Lillian Laurie,

You wonder that women cry out so against their fate, but I do not wonder. Of course some suffer more than others but after having "one" child there is no women who does not dread having another, it is not only the suffering at the time, but has so many little attendant ills that with some, are a constant annoyance and trouble, even with a good husband who sympathizes and understands, it is not all sunshine. It is then we find the penalty we pay for love. It is all at once the greatest pain and the greatest pleasure, that a childless woman never knows. Then take the poor tired mother of the farm or the working class, with but one pair of hands to do everything and they are the ones who have the largest families and the smallest wage to make both ends meet; either the housework or the children must be neglected, and both are generally half cared for. She can't do everything as it should, even if she wanted, such a life is misery, and I don't wonder they wish they knew how to restrict their family to suit their means. It should be so. It would be a great deal better for a woman to raise say four to six healthy children than eight to ten, spindling, delicate ones, half of whom die, after all the trouble of partly rearing them. Of course some women raise large families of healthy children, but not the majority. I think every poor working couple should have the knowledge so as to have families to suit the income, and not as it now is, the woman of means and leisure is the one who has no family or only one or two when she is better able to have more who can blame the poor and middle class, it is more the care and expense of rearing children should be looked at not only of having them.

The bishops of the recent synod said it was to be regretted that the restriction of families was prevalent, how many of our ministers restrict their families? I know of several who have. Some may say they receive too small a salary to rear a large one, doesn't that same answer do for the poor man of toil, with small pay? I think so, now I do not advocate the one child business, I believe we should look after the interest of our race and keep up our end of it and not allow the yellow or any other race to overcome us, but we should be moderate in all things, even to having children, then our women would be healthier and happier, and how much more time would the little ones get. Who has not seen the tired mother of 9 or ten, one in arms, another tugging at her skirt who should be in arms, the rest scattered here and there like promiscuous furniture, untidy, dirty, all kinds of work that should be done left undone, it breaks the heart. Then see my lady of leisure with one or two saunter down the street, and in most cases she looks down on her unfortunate sister, would she help, she might lessen some of this.

Now I have written a rather long winded letter, but it is something I often think about and would help if I knew how, but must not take up more of your valuable time, so close.

Remaining sincerely yours,

NAWITKA

Plate 7. A tea party at Ed McDonald's Flee Island farm, 1905 (John Cowell Coll. 35, Provincial Archives of Manitoba [N 19584]).

Plate 8. Binding wire grass, Vita, Manitoba, 1915 (W. J. Sisler Coll. 192, Provincial Archives of Manitoba [N 9607]).

Plate 9. The cooks at a lumbering operation, Riding Mountain, Manitoba, 1905 (Robert Lindsay Coll. 6, Provincial Archives of Manitoba [N 17291]).

Plate 10. Marco and Maria Bussanich on an early "double ender" fish boat, 1920 (Delta Museum and Archives, Delta, British Columbia [1980-52-69]).

Plate 11. Board of Directors of the Saskatchewan Grain Growers' Association—Women's Section, at the Fifth Annual Convention, February 12-15, 1918, outside First Baptist Church, Regina (Saskatchewan Archives Board [R-B4481]).

Plate 12. Evelyn Lord (seated) and Leila Lord working in the local telephone exchange, 1912 (Delta Museum and Archives, Delta, British Columbia [1970-1-494]).

Plate 13. Presentation of a petition by a delegation of the Political Equality League for the enfranchisement of women. Lillian Beynon Thomas (Lillian Laurie), woman's editor, *Free Press Prairie Farmer* (1906-1917), is the woman in back right, December 23, 1915 (Events Coll. 173/3, Provincial Archives of Manitoba [N 9905]).

PRIM ROSE AT HOME, *Family Herald and Weekly Star*
December 22, 1909

THE FRANCHISE

Dear Prim Rose:

I was pleased to see that the question of extending the franchise to the feminine half of the population has come up for discussion. I think there is reason to believe that this would be not only an act of justice to women, but of real benefit to mankind. Whatever may have been the standard of morality or intelligence of women of the past, it is certainly equal to that of man at present, and I think both have been equal for many years. We have only to pick up any late paper to read of some woman distinguishing herself, and even excelling in some line not hitherto followed by her sex. If the vote is a means of protecting one's interests, it cannot be right that the weaker should be deprived of protection, but reforms often come slowly, and they usually meet opposition. It is pleasing to know, however, that many men favor the vote for woman, thinking that women's influence is usually for good. That a woman's place is at home is true. It is also true that a man's place is where his work keeps him, yet both have an equal right to the benefit of just laws, and an unrepresented class cannot expect justice. I have never been able to decide in my own mind, whether women should or should not hold office. I think there is so much time occupied in training the children (work which should not be relegated by parents to others), that women could not in the majority of cases give the time required, though I have read of women filling public offices satisfactorily. I was struck with the remark a man made once when I asked him if he thought women should be privileged to vote, he said he did not consider the vote a privilege, but a right, and a right belonging to every adult.

I notice by the letters the Dower Law is still receiving some thought. In this country, where a woman has no legal share in the home or income, some men deed a portion of their property to the wife. A man cannot be hindered then in his business, but it is, of course only the appreciative husband who does so. The wife of the unjust man is without remuneration. With sincere good wishes to all,

Alberta   A WIFE AND MOTHER

HOME LOVING HEARTS, *Free Press Prairie Farmer*
January 12, 1910

A VEXED QUESTION

Dear Miss Laurie:

May I, too, have a small corner of your valuable page? I have been a reader of the Weekly Free Press and consider it a very interesting paper.

I liked A Widow's letter very much. I, too, think women should stand together more. Almond Rock you have touched the right key. I hope to see more follow your example. Then there will be less family jars. I do not agree with Rich in Rope, not telling the children all, not giving them a proper knowledge of life. Why not? Who is better fitted to fill the most sacred of duties more beautifully than a loving and companionable mother to her daughters? The father his sons? The children fully trusting and believing their parents will not listen to the vulgar form they receive the knowledge in from their companions at school and on the streets. The half of our dear young girls who are being led astray and cast aside can lay the blame at their mother's door for improper teaching. There are numerous good books such as the Self and Sex series that should be in every home where young girls and boys are growing up. Mothers, be honest to your children, for it is only when the mistaken ideas and false modesty are done away with that we will have better young man and women.

I have numerous patterns for a little girl's dresses one or two years old, and pants and blouse patterns for a boy of four. Also a good pair of boy's boots, No. 3. They are too small for my boy. Will exchange for reading matter. Now Miss Laurie, hoping you will take me under your family wing, will close, with best wishes of the season to all.

Saskatchewan   ADDARIAH

Addariah—Sure, you are received into the circle, but I may not be able to shelter you from those who do not believe as you do about telling boys and girls about life. Many do not favor it. They appear to think that in that case, knowledge is not power. Only you mothers can test the matter.—L.L.

FIRESIDE, *Grain Growers' Guide*
March 23, 1910

A REAL GRIEVANCE

Dear Editor:—

I am a constant reader of your Guide, so please allow me a small space.

I am a farmer's wife and would like to say a little about a farmer's wife in threshing time.

We farm about 640 acres and have quite a lot of work to do, and you are well aware that female assistance is very difficult to procure, and allow me to say that when threshing time comes around a farmer's wife has to work and cook for twenty-five men as a rule, and only one woman to help, and the hour for men to get out in the morning to the mill is about seven o'clock and very often half past seven, and I have seen the mill very often not start until eight o'clock. Of course, no matter to the woman! In they come at twelve o'clock as hungry as hounds and the woman has to have everything ready in a minute. And if they would hurry back to their work the way they hurry in—but, no! A shrink here and a dodge there. But, hold on, it is not three o'clock until they are looking for lunch and the lunch has to be iced cakes and hot buns. Now, Mr.Editor, that is not all, but we have one thresher in our community who sent word he would be at a house on a Saturday to thresh for one hour before supper, but did not show up till the hour of ten o'clock and they expected the woman of the house to be up and have their supper ready. I don't think a woman should be expected to do all this. A woman is a complete slave on the farm, working after men. Also women work and cook all day Sunday (rainy days included) for these men who lay up in the caboose and smoke and have a good rest; in fact, it's got nowadays that threshers expect a small banquet three times a day, and a lunch in between. It's only in this part where the lunch business exists.

I really think that men in Manitoba look forward to threshing time for a filling out, especially men who have no housekeepers. The idea of hearty men wanting lunch when they get three good meals in the day!

Hoping, Mr. Editor, I have not taken up too much of your space in your valuable paper. Might I say I would be pleased to hear some other farmer's wife's views on this.

Yours truly,

Belleview   FARMER'S WIFE (SLAVE)

HOME LOVING HEARTS, *Free Press Prairie Farmer*
May 1, 1910

STORY OF A MATERNITY NURSE

Dear Editor

Perhaps a nurse in the backwoods and prairie may be of some use. I have worked in the field for eleven years next April, the nearest doctor being 15 miles away. Sometimes my patients are 30 miles or more from a doctor. I am English, had a training in England, but am not certified.

I have faced storms of every kind in Manitoba. I have left home at every inconvenient season of the year, also a young family of my own. I have also been credited with saving many lives. In these eleven years I have never lost a patient, and only two stillborn babies. In only three cases did I have a doctor called, but often I am in correspondence when I fear a case may prove fatal. I have taken them in and cared for them in my own home, also in many instances provided bedding, night dresses and something to wrap the little arrival in to save its life. I have also, to save a woman's life, taken sufficient nourishment to give strength to struggle through the trying time. To those suffering from accidents, cuts, illnesses of different kinds do I also give ointment, powders, pills, and advice. To those in poverty need I say it is free. I receive no help from anyone. I am also a very poor woman, and often I have not had covering to keep myself warm or anything approaching it. Often when there is only one room for everything, and everybody together, with a moderately large family as onlookers, I take two sheets and make a private bed. I was to one such case where there were already five children, each wearing one long garment, no boots or stockings, no food in the house, no light when darkness came on. I was alone except for an unseen power. No one could speak English except myself. Some neighbors brought in food from their scant homes; another lent a well-filled lamp.

In another family, only one room, five children, the oldest being only seven years old, two were born in the same year (and not twins). I had my own little one with me. The two oldest were taken to a neighbor, and in the earliest hours of morning in January you might have heard five children, my own included, all crying pitifully, and no other woman there, only the husband and father, and none of these little ones understood one word of English. I provided sheets round the bed, bedding, etc. and in that house there was not the price of a stamp for a letter. I gave of my scant food and all I possessed, $1.00, not knowing when or how I could replace it. I left bread in the dough and no one at home, hours of waiting, and the bread I could not afford to spoil, for truly I had little enough. I got the man to go to my house and pull it on a hand sleigh to a house three quarters of a mile away to be baked, and I was thankful I was able to eat it and digest it. It is only on rare occasions I ever have another woman with me. Some of the patients pay me, and some pay me more than I earn out of gratitude, and with these included, my whole income averages from $30 to $50 per year, from Jan. 1 to Dec. 31. In one year I almost reached $80. This was the most I ever made in one year. I have never received more that $15 from any one case, and gone every day to attend and do all for the mothers and children. In these cases they were really cases for a doctor, and to make sure the patient was not neglected, I went myself, and only on one occasion did I reach the sum of $15.

Now if anyone cares to come in here an take up my work, I will retire and give all the advice that it is possible free, and help in any way I can to assist the woman who will step in. Also, necessity was the mother of invention. I may also add, if anyone wishes to know a true fact, "Maternity complete without a wash day," I will write once for all how to do it, but it could not be published in these pages, and if the editor will undertake, after I explain it, to deliver it, I will gladly do so. I have a family of my own, and never had a woman or girl to do one hour's work or washing day. I am always too poor myself.

My address is with the editor, if anyone doubts these facts come and see me, and don't expect any luxury, for I don't possess any. And please don't think I have no home troubles. Some people think they have hardships, but sometimes I have iron ships to contend with. I could go on, but let me say in conclusion that I never allow anyone to know I lend or give except the one interested. It hurts.

With best wishes to all, and to those who will come out into the field, I sign myself, once more,

FARMER'S WIFE

Farmer's Wife—You surely do know what hardship is, and I am sure your help could not be valued in money. It must be a great thing to know that you have saved lives, and brought cheer and hope and comfort to so many. I hope I may meet you some day.

PRIM ROSE AT HOME, *Family Herald and Weekly Star*
August 24, 1910

WHY YOUNG PEOPLE LEAVE THE FARM

Dear Prim Rose:

The cry is going up loud and long that girls and boys are leaving the farms.

Is it any wonder that the farms are losing and the city gains? What are they on the farms but the unpaid drudge of the father? not even getting paid in love and caresses; for of all the farmer's homes that I ever visited, I have yet to see the father that lavished open affection on his sons and daughters. He seems to think that to give them food and shelter with an occasional new dress, suit, or hat is enough. He shows as much affection to his cattle and pigs as to his sons and daughters. You never see his wife or grown daughters being petted or caressed, and I have often pitied him; because that selfish, stolid nature has missed the soft tenderness that the true woman so loves to bestow when not chilled into reserve.

I think of the home of the highly educated, the cultured and refined, and I see the loving glances of the fond parents as a son or daughter enter their presence, or the fond stroke of the hand as it caresses the head, or pats the hand that is laid on the shoulder or knee, the loving kiss of wife or daughter as they stoop to give the caress that is a joy both to give and receive, that it is "twice blessed"; and then I think of the barren hearts in all the farmer's homes I ever knew, for in them I never saw any demonstrations of affection; no outward and visible sign of inward love that is so beautiful in families, that knits them together with ties that are "hooks of steel."

What inducement is there to the boys and girl to stay on the farm where they are nothing more than servants, and wear out their lives in the poorest of all poorly paid service.

The energy that is spent from daylight to dark on the farm in the most sordid and monotonous dullness, if expanded properly in the city would give three times the results both financially and mentally, and it is the lack of mental refreshment on the farm that tells the hardest on the tired mother and girls. When night comes they are dead tired from the same old routine, but there in no bright mental relaxation.

But instead of bewailing the fact that the girls and boys leave the farm, endeavor to make the farm a cheerful, happy home. Put love—not merely the love that the brute parent has for its young—but real love, tenderness, caresses, into your lives. Let your wife and daughter be more than servants: don't let them drag through life weary eyed, worn out, heavy of step. As your finances allow of it don't spend every cent that you don't bank on more stock and acres that will cause more work for the already over-worked woman; spend some of it for a servant and let the woman get some rest.

But nine times out of ten farmers seem to think that all a wife is for is to save servant hire; and in such eyes a woman's good qualities are graded by her capacity to work. Can you wonder that as girls grow up in this more enlightened day that they refuse to be made dumb beasts of burden as their poor mothers are?

They go to school and education fits them for more than milk-maids and cooks with not even warm ties of tenderness and affection to keep them happy. In fact, it appears to the thinker that if a man had in his soul the rich quality of tenderness and display of affection he would not make household slaves of his wife and children.

So what is to be done? Mothers, it lies with you. Rome was not built in a day, and just so it will take a generation to start things aright.

The standard of the highest civilization is gauged by the esteem in which its women are held; so to reach this, teach your boys from infancy to be gentlemen; teach them kindness, thoughtfulness, consideration; above all teach them to be considerate and courteous to their sisters.

Remember, each mother of a son, that you are raising a husband to some woman like yourself; a father to daughters like your own.

It depends on you to raise one thoughtless, selfish, despotic, or one such as you wish yours would be.

No wives and daughters in the world are more to be envied than those of the Southern planters. They too live in the country, but is like the old nobility of England. The wife and daughters are treated like queens, and the sons are made loved companions.

No work of any description is ever expected of the womankind, the wife is the true wife, the soulmate, the intellectual companion—not the servant, but like the chatelaine of the old baronial castle, and the sons and daughters are as the cornerstones of a palace. Of course, you say, "Yes, but on those southern plantations there are hundreds of negroes with overseers to superintend, etc., etc." Quite true, but—and just here is the point—if the Southern gentlemen had not been taught by his parents to render homage to all women, simply because of their womanhood, to protect them from all hardships, to feel the highest reverence for them because his mother was a woman; because the mother of God was a woman; because the world owes all it is, ever was, ever shall be to woman; her influence, her love, her suffering by which man enters, upon his very being, if this reverence had not been instilled, he too would have looked on woman in the ignorant half-heathenish way—as only a servant, or at best, a housekeeper.

So mothers, the future of the farmer's wife and daughter lies with you; teach your sons from infancy to be gentlemen, and no man can be a gentlemen who only looks on a woman as a servant. Teach him to honor and respect women from the very fact that she is the gentler, tenderer sex, to be protected and sheltered; and that a good woman is "far above rubies."

With chivalry in the hearts of your son there will be a different life in store for the future farmer's wife and daughter.

British Columbia   ONE WHO KNOWS

INGLE NOOK, *The Farmer's Advocate*
October 12, 1910

COMFORT WANTED

Dear Dame Durden:

We have taken The Advocate about a year and I don't think I ever read a better paper. As I was standing in my kitchen all alone washing, just now, my heart was made to ache. I saw two women pass, about a quarter of a mile from our house, going towards town, which is ten miles from here. I suppose they were women that live within two or three miles of us, though I couldn't just recognize them from here. One was in a democrat by herself; the other in a buggy, also by herself. How I would liked to have gone with them for a ride! But they didn't even look towards the house, just kept laying the whip to the horses, as if they couldn't go fast enough. I never get to go off the place scarcely, just stay home and attend to the stock, while my husband goes with the thresher and other places to make money. We came here about a year and a half ago from one of the middle states, where we were born and raised. We bought a half of a quarter section of land without seeing it; paid too much for it, and paid cash. We laid out about fifteen hundred for stock and farming implements. We have a good two storey house, but haven't fixed it up on the inside much yet, as we are very dissatisfied and might leave any time. It seems to me people regard us as very poor people. The most of them came once. I had met some of them at one of the neighbor's houses and noticed they played cards most of the time. I told them I didn't know how to play, and I didn't think I would like the game anyway. So I didn't have any cards for them when they called on me. I entertained the best I could under the circumstances, but it seemed the day was very dull for them. I was used to music and singing and talking where I came from. I sold my organ and all my nice furniture back East, and you may be sure I miss it all. But I had my big oak heater shipped here and bought a new cooking stove, iron bedstead, one rocker and some other things, and keep my naked floors scrubbed white and am considered a good cook. So I don't understand why we are slighted even if we don't ride in a rubber-tired buggy or automobile. We had the telephone, R.F.D. of mail, lived within six miles of a large city, and have lived in Pueblo, Colo., Missoula, Mont., and other like places, but never ran across one like this. It is true we have two good neighbors, but they have several little children and can't come often. Is it possible some people can't be interested only with cards? I thought at first with all the hard work, and loneliness, I would surely die or go insane, and I believe I would only for the Bible and your paper.

In-the-Depths

You poor, dear, lonesome soul. I just ached for you when reading your letter. Don't you get discouraged—two good neighbors is a pretty fair start and the others will come sooner or later. Be kind and jolly when you meet them and they will soon wonder why they didn't long ago cultivate the acquaintance of such a bright little woman as you. I do think that constant card playing is a destroyer of conversation, but perhaps it kills gossip as well as conversation on good subjects. Unless you have conscientious scruples about cards, why not learn to play a little? That will bring you into touch with your neighbors and you can edge in the music and books and things you are interested in. Then some time send them a laughing invitation to an evening without cards. Get somebody to read or tell a funny story, somebody to play the guitar or violin or even the mouth organ, while everybody sings and have some good games. They will go home declaring what a good time they had.

I wish you had sent me your full address and I'd have sent a message to cheer you up a little before you can see this. Come again, Friend o' Mine, and bring your troubles. Don't stay in the depths alone. And don't get the idea in your mind that the neighbors are slighting you on purpose.

That is fatal to happiness. They are thoughtless, that's all; though we know that
> *"Evil is wrought by want of thought*
> *As well as by want of heart."*
Cheer up. —*D.D.*

PRIM ROSE AT HOME. *Family Herald and Weekly Star*
November 2, 1910

LOCAL OPTION

Dear Prim Rose:

If you have room in your valuable column for still another bachelor to have a say, I would like to join your interesting discussions.

Now the Local Option is so prominently before the electors of Canada, I think it is a good subject, and one on which much may be said to benefit us all.

In every town or district where this vote is placed before the people, a great responsibility is laid on every voter, and not only the voters; but on every individual who can in any way influence a voter in the right way.

There is a great agitation abroad at present in favor of votes for women but if every woman in Canada who has any influence at all, (and where is the one who hasn't) would use that influence to gain for her country freedom from the chains of the greatest slavery that ever bound any fair land, the result of this great struggle is sure to be victory for right.

Here is a golden opportunity for married women to exert their influence with husband or son.

Nor is the opportunity confined to the married women, it extends equally to the unmarried.

Sister, you have brothers! Do you realize how the clasp of the hand and a beseeching word from you may change the mark he is about to make? Don't fail to do your all!

Girls, you have sweethearts who are seeking from you the greatest gift a woman can give—her love! Do you know how he, who loudly protests he will do anything for you, is going to mark his ballot? Have you drawn him out on this important subject? Are you testing him? It is

your opportunity, and see to it, that if he is not loyal to this great temperance movement, and that with a full, true heart. I repeat, "see to it,"
that you assert your noble womanhood and protect yourself and your
home from any danger from liquor's curse before it is too late.

It is an opportunity for man and women alike that may not return.

Much can be said on this all-important question and if any of the
readers would like to exchange ideas, privately with a man of thirty, he
would be pleased to reply, and I will refer you to our kind Prim Rose for
my address.

Alberta   TEMPERANCE WORKER

HOME JOURNAL, *The Farmer's Advocate*
December 4, 1910

OLD MAIDS

*It is with spinsterhood as with greatness; some are born old maids, some
achieve old maidenhood and some have single blessedness thrust upon
them. Unlike poets, old maids are both born and made.*

*With the born old maids, years have nothing to do. They were pre-
destined to that state from the cradle, and were as firmly settled in it at
thirteen as at thirty or forty. Some of them married, too, but that did not
work any change. They merely left their native element for one not suited
to them. Until the day of death, they are actively conscious of being
wrongly placed and uncomfortable, if not actively unhappy. It is the misfortune of their temperament, not their fault.*

*Achieving spinsterhood can be accomplished in various ways. The
flirt and coquette attain to it in surprise, as every effort was being made
for the opposite result. They were fascinating instead of attractive, and
overdid it. The bad tempered often achieve it, unless they marry upon
short acquaintance; and that also, is the only thing that saves the selfish
and untidy girls from wearing their own names all through life. Thus
originates the peevish and sour visaged old maid, who forms a very small
proportion of the whole class, in spite of paragraphers and cartoonists.*

*The third class are the most to be pitied, and yet they do not want
pity, merely sympathetic comprehension and friendliness. The single
state has been thrust upon them. They knew themselves fitted for the jobs
of wifehood and motherhood, yet had to relinquish the hope of them. In*

some cases they were located in tiny villages or in the wilds where there were no marriageable men. As a girl once wrote pathetically, regarding matrimonial bureaus. Who is coming forty miles over a rough mountain road to court me? Then there are girls whose sense of duty and responsibility makes them give up the claims of love. To wait upon enfeebled parents, to care for motherless brothers and sisters, or to be mother to a brother's orphaned flock, many a girl has given up her lover.

PRIM ROSE AT HOME, *Family Herald and Weekly Star*
January 11, 1911

GRAHAM ISLAND

Dear Prim Rose,

Would you be interested in Graham Island of the Queen Charlotte Group? This island is the most northerly one of the group and Skidegate Harbor—with the towns of Graham City and Queen Charlotte City, and the Indian village of Skidegate, is only 90 miles from Prince Rupert, across the Straits of Hecate. Those straits have, only recently, been one of the causes of the arbitration between the States and Canada. They teem with fish of the commercial varieties and provide one of the tributary assets of our island. The island has considerable mineral wealth, scarcely prospected, but including the rich ores of "Southbaster," within a couple of miles of Skidegate harbor, and assaying as much as $2000 to the ton, and the placer mines of the eastern beach. The later gold is found in magnetic iron (black sand), and though not extremely rich, yields good wages to the three or four small outfits now working there.

Another asset of considerable value is our easily accessible merchantable timber. The hills on the south and west of the island are covered with fine spruce, hemlock, cedar, including yellow cedar (worth $60 to $100 per thousand). At present little is being milled.

Fully half the island is now held by timber limits and coal license, but there is still a considerable area open to pre-emption. The soil is usually rich vegetable mould on clay or sand subsoil and the greater part will require draining as well as clearing. The timber of the lower leveler parts except in the vicinity of the beach and along the streams is usually second growth with small stuff interspersed with many ancient windfalls. Occasionally one finds small meadows of boggy nature and in the interior east of Masset Inlet are immense muskegs. It will take thousands of dollars to reclaim these latter. Along the eastern beach from Tel-lel River to Rose Spit, is a strip of open park land ranging five to twenty chains in width, bearing a heavy growth of grass—sufficient to provide a range for three or four "critters" necessary for the comfort and convenience of every settler along the coast, and in this fifty or sixty miles there are not a dozen settlers. True, we are handicapped by the lack of roads or trails, but there is a fair pack trail Skidegate to Tel-lel River and the beach is passable thence clear to Masset. We are working for and expect to get a road up the east coast the coming summer. Considerable misunderstanding has prevailed even among the older settlers by the persistent rumor that ten chains along the beach has been reserved for wind break and for road purposes, but this rumor has been disposed of. It was evidently started to keep out settlers, as the strip along the beach is the most desirable land on practically each individual holding.

Now I am coming to the climate, the greatest asset of them all! We have the ideal climate, for one with leisure at least. This far, November 25, the coldest weather recorded has been 29 degrees Fahrenheit. Zero weather is practically unknown. Considerable snow falls in the interior and the higher altitudes but near the beach this is usually seen in the form of rain and even if it does snow seldom lies any length of time. That is why it is possible to range cattle here the year around and why wild cattle could live and multiply here. There were at one time large numbers of these latter here, but the hunters have practically exterminated them. Beef has always maintained a good price here and for a matter of about eight years these same "wild bulls," as they are called locally, have been butchered to meet the demands of the market. Oh, yes, our summer weather! "Not so worse." We have a considerable rainfall, it is true, but we have no excessive heat—76 degrees in the shade was the hottest weather my thermometer recorded last summer, and the prevailing noon temperature was between 55 and 70 degrees F, and summer frosts are unknown. Garden truck and small fruits make excellent growth, and apples have matured. Tree fruits have really not been experimented with enough to justify assertions pro or con.

British Columbia   Settler

HOME LOVING HEARTS, *Free Press Prairie Farmer*
February 7, 1912

TIRED'S LETTER OF THANKS

Dear Miss Lillian Laurie:

I received your letter with the $11, and there was another letter before Christmas with ten dollars and no name; and one dear sister sent me $5, and there have been letters with one dollar and $2. I have received $32.00 altogether, and two sisters sent me such beautiful clothes. They were Mrs. John Lundy and Mrs. Aikenhead, and I do not have words to thank them. This big sum of money frightens me. God knows I will gladly try to be a neighbor if I ever have the means and indeed I have tried in my little way before, but it was so little I was able to do.

Dear Miss Laurie, will you please do me one kindness more? Will you thank them for me, for their lovely letters, so good and hopeful, and the great help they have given me. You always have the right words to say, but my heart is so full I forget the little I ever knew of English. Dear Miss Laurie please do, and God bless your goodness for all this help is through you and I will always pray for your happiness when I look on my little ones. Goodbye.

TIRED

Tired—I feel that your letter is the best thanks those have helped you can have. L.L.

HOME LOVING HEARTS, *Free Press Prairie Farmer*
July 2, 1912

A HELPFUL LETTER

My Dear Miss Laurie:

I do enjoy the page for women so much, so many helpful hints and suggestions in it.

Someone asks how to make homemade beer, or hop ale. I take 13 packages of hops and tie them in a cheesecloth sack, also 2 cups of cornmeal in another and put them in a large kettle of water and boil about half an hour. Then I take out the bags and set the water off to cool; when lukewarm I put a yeast cake in and let stand for 4 hours, when it will be ready to bottle. About 5 gallons of water is required, and by adding 2 tablespoons of ginger, or four or five lemons, a most delicious wholesome drink will be the result. A member also asks for directions to make sauerkraut. Cut or chop the cabbage fine, then into your keg or barrel put a generous layer of the cabbage, and then sparingly of salt, use just enough salt to season the whole thing right, by sprinkling it on the layers as it goes in, and mash it down tight. Keep mashing or pounding till the brine is drawn out of the cabbage, and covers the whole, then put a heavy weight on it with a clean flour sack beneath it, spread over the cabbage to keep out the dirt and flies and set away. If kept in a warm place it ought to be sour in two weeks.

I see where one member suffered so much with rheumatism and nothing helped but an electric belt. I have a simple remedy which I hope those affected will try. Take a teaspoonful of cream of tartar and sulphur, of each one-half teaspoonful for three mornings, the first thing in the morning, and then omit three mornings, and take again for three, until you have taken it nine mornings, then quit, if after a week or ten days you still have any pain, start it as before. This is so simple that I'm afraid very few will try, but I have yet to see its equal as a remedy for rheumatism.

I make a self-rising dumpling that my mother made ever since I can remember, and my children are so fond of them that I must ask the sisters to try them. To two cupfuls of flour, 1 teaspoon of salt, and an egg mixed with milk or water. I put them in potato soup or beef soup and always have a dish full with sauerkraut. When the mixture has set, say one hour, and dinner is about ready to serve, I cut them off with a sharp knife into some boiling water and dip the knife into the water occasionally to keep them from sticking to it.

There is a root which grows up here everywhere in the woods, that is so good for confinement. Its use started with the Indians, but the white people use it here, and declare it a Godsend. If I can find out the name of it, will send it for the sake of the poor women who are so far from help. Do you know Miss Laurie, where I might send some of it to learn its name?

When I read the letters of the different women my heart aches for them, and I often look in vain (and I am glad of it too) that their lot is not as bad as mine, but complaining helps no one, and the only thing left to do is to brace up against all odds, and bear it, hoping for something better in the future.

I live in British Columbia, Cariboo, a very hilly, wooded place, very little farming is done here as yet, and living is enormous. Eggs have been $1.25 all winter, fresh pork, when it can be had, and mutton too, is 25 cents per lb., bacon 47 cents per lb., dried fruits 25 cents per lb., and other things in proportion.

If this is too long, or you don't see fit, just put it, you know where.

Wishing one and all a bright and prosperous year.

I am yours sincerely,

CHRISTINA

PRIM ROSE AT HOME, *Family Herald and Weekly Star*
October 30, 1912

HER HEART'S DESIRE

Dear Prim Rose,

Will you extend the courtesy of your columns to help a young spinster from England, whom circumstances in this country have shut [her] out from the society she once enjoyed there.

Orphaned, but equipped with an excellent education, the said young spinster—myself—set out for Canada to teach for a livelihood, alone, but backed up by excellent testimonials, and references. I have succeeded, but, I am now 28, and the future looms ahead of me, with the sole prospect of teaching from morning till night, the rest of my days. I have neither leisure nor opportunity, for society, and so cannot hope to make acquaintances. It therefore appears I shall some day be shelved as an old maid, unless I take steps which certainly appear most unconventional, but are, I think, justified by the conditions. I am sure if some of well-educated bachelor readers, or even widowers, who are in quest of a good wife, would exchange a few letters with me, mutual advantage would arise to one of them. I am in B.C. but should be pleased to hear from any other province. I know for a certainty so it is barely vanity to assert it, that my education and training have placed me above the average girl, and that I possess the attributes which go to make an excellent partner in organizing and managing a happy peaceful home, and, I believe, and know, that two of the some mind, can make existence for each other an earthly Paradise.

In the hope that you will do me the favor I ask, I enclose my name and address, for your use only.

I am, dear Prim Rose, yours faithfully and in anticipation gratefully,

British Columbia   PENELOPE

HOME LOVING HEARTS, *Free Press Prairie Farmer*
December 18, 1912

CHILDREN NEED A HOME

Dear Lillian Laurie,

Can I find a small space in your corner page. I have just started again to get the Free Press, for I like it most for the woman's page. Well, I am wanting to hear from some kind lonely couple who would like to take care of my two children, or one of them. They are very pretty sweet children. The boy is turned 6 years old and the girl is turned 3 years old. Why I would like to get them in a private home in Alberta or southern Saskatchewan is that being used to the high dry climate the coast here is not suitable for them, and catching cold as they have done since they came here, would leave me with two sickly children. I have to make my own living so far, and they get neglected as my husband is in the insane asylum a long time since. I could spare a little pay for the two and I can keep them in warm clothes, as I can get out to work and get more pay that way. A lady in British Columbia can get from $30 to $40 a month. I have a small baby six months old I can get someone here to mind, or perhaps I can take her with me. I noticed a lady asking for a little girl in your October number. Well, my letter is long and I hope to get a space soon, as I would like them in a nice home before it got too cold to send them. I will send a picture of them to anyone who would like to see them, as some people would like nice children. They are both healthy. My address is with the editor.

FLYNN VALLEY

PRIM ROSE AT HOME, *Family Herald and Weekly Star*
December 25, 1912

A PRAIRIE CHRISTMAS TREE

Dear Prim Rose:

We spent Christmas in Manitoba thirty-five years ago, when there was no railroad into Winnipeg. We went with oxen and waggon to a neighbour's five miles away, and took our Christmas dinner there.

Eight years ago we went into a new part of Saskatchewan. At Christmas time we decided to hold our Sunday School entertainment on Christmas Day, as there were so many young bachelors there. The young men said if they bought the turkeys would we do the cooking? Of course we said yes. It made it more Christmasy. We had four turkeys to cook. We could not have plum pudding, but had mince and other pies and cakes, etc. Over fifty sat down to dinner, and everyone enjoyed it immensely.

Now for the Christmas tree part. We were on the prairie and not a tree in sight. The boys went to the sand hills and got some ground cedar, then the boys and girls came the night before and built up a tree and decorated the house. You will be wondering what we got to put on it. Well, we sent to town for toys and candies and some of the other things we made. I wish you could have seen that tree! It looked good to the little ones away on the prairie. It made work for some of us, but oh! the joy of doing something for the little ones.

My best wishes to all for a very happy Christmas and New Year.

Saskatchewan   ROSEBUSH

HOME LOVING HEARTS, *Free Press Prairie Farmer*
December 25, 1912

THINGS LOOK BLACK

Dear Miss Laurie,

I am so much interested in your valuable page. I just love it. I wish to thank "Dutch" for the excellent candy recipes she sent. I tried them and they were good; also I thank "Nebraska Golden Rod" for her "raisin pie" recipe. It was certainly unique, and the best I ever tasted.

Also last, but not least, I thank "Penelope, Sask." for her bright helpful letters, and her good recipes. I think she is a woman with a good heart and tries to make this dull world of ours a little brighter. It certainly is drab enough sometimes for us prairie women. Three years ago we homesteaded here and everything has turned out wrong. First year three oxen died and no crop; second year 3 horses died and dried out crop; third year, hailed out, and the bit we saved not threshed till this spring. It was only the seed we saved and when it was seeded it never came up—not a blade. Seemingly the germ was killed, being out all winter. It seems no good depending entirely on one's crop, so I'm going to try and raise chickens next year if all goes well. I wonder if any of the better-fixed sisters have an incubator for sale. Just a small one to try my hand on first; I'm Scotch and cautious. I always make Robert Bruce's watch-word mine—"Mak Linar" I make sure. I am a firm believer in the divine law and women's suffrage, always have been. I feel very down-hearted tonight. I've just discovered (quite by accident) that my husband has mortgaged our homestead and the money all paid away. I've worked hand in hand with him night and day.

It is a great shame that a man is allowed to sign away everything like that. I've always been so much against it; yet a man can do it unknown to his wife. I have raised chickens each year by mother hens, but not enough to sell. I want to try and make some money. I should be so glad of suggestions from some of the "old-timers." Flour this year was quite an item with us, so I bought a little grist mill at Eaton's and ground down some of our hailed wheat that the elevators would not buy, and mixed it half and half with flour, and it made excellent brown bread. I make batter with the flour and then knead in with the ground wheat.

Thanking you, dear Miss Laurie, for your past kindnesses, I am

Saskatchewan   BETTY

P.S.—I endorse one of the member's suggestion: "That if any of the sisters has anything good to give in the shape of recipes or hints, etc., etc., that they should be printed in the page." I often see something I should like to try and when I have to write for it perhaps wait for 3 or 4 weeks for reply, the necessity of wanting it is over, and often as not we busy folk have no time to write and the post office is far away. I'm sure it would lighten our dear editor's labors quite a lot, not speaking of ourselves.

BETTY

PRIM ROSE AT HOME, *Family Herald and Weekly Star*
December 25, 1912

A CHRISTMAS TREE

Dear Prim Rose,

I am taking advantage of your request for the Christmas number, telling how we spent Christmas one year. It carries me back thirty years ago.

I was always in favor of a tree for the children, but had not before attained my desire. That year my husband and I felt we must have one, so preparations were made in good time. My husband went to the nearest swamp and cut down a good-sized tamarack, bringing it home on the sleigh. In the meantime, I bought the presents and trimmings. In those days Christmas trees were rare in our vicinity, so we invited all the children in the neighborhood. If I remember right, seventeen children, and several grown-ups responded to our invitation. It was a beautiful day, with just enough snow for sleighing. The children came early in the afternoon and what fun they had. We had a field almost covered with ice, grand for skating and sliding, and they made the welkin ring with their merry voices. Then came supper, a bounteous one it was. The children were served first, and needless to say they did justice to the good things, with their appetites sharpened by the outdoor exercises. But whoever saw hearty boys and girls fail at the table, bless them? Then, after supper they played games in the big kitchen. The children all did what they could in entertaining. Our youngest child, four years, got up on a chair and recited "Little Jack Horner," then we all clapped hands, as he did so. He has been reciting to larger crowds many times since then.

At last came the crowning glory of the day. It was a surprise to the children when the door was opened. The "Oh's" and "My's" were many and their delight was boundless in seeing the lovely tree brilliantly lighted and loaded with gifts. After some time the tree was dismantled, everyone receiving a present. My husband acted as Santa. Then the big sleigh fellow sang, "Hate is strong and mocks the song of peace on earth, good will to men." But though indeed, there is much evil in the world to-day, yet there are many signs of the coming of that "divine far-off event toward which the whole creation moves."

Let us take a brief look at the world today and see how the cause of universal peace is progressing. On this side of the water we are soon to celebrate the completion of a hundred years of peace between the United States, Great Britain and Canada. Surely this is a record of which we may well be proud.

After all, it is individual peace that will bring about national and world wide peace.

All over this broad Dominion there are men and women to whom Christmas brings tender and pleasant memories, but who do not look forward with pleasurable anticipation to this Christmas season, because they are far from the old home among strangers and no one has offered them hospitality. Perhaps we can reach some of these with a spirit of good fellowship and cheer.

A Merry Christmas and a Happy New Year.

MORNING ALBERTAN

PRIM ROSE AT HOME, *Family Herald and Weekly Star*
April 9, 1913

MATRIMONIAL LAWS IN SASKATCHEWAN

Dear Prim Rose:

Since many of the readers seem to have the "dare" spirit when it comes to matrimony, I would like to point out that in this Province of Saskatchewan there is a certain law in force, which possibly it might be someone's duty to point out since, indeed 'tis a strange and extraordinary law. It declares, in effect, that "a man may die and by virtue of a will, wherein his will is clearly so expressed his wife after his death may not lawfully claim or own a part, or a part of a part of his estate, nor may she obtain possession of one cent of his money." It is apparent that this law, as it stands, justifies any man who at his death may leave his wife absolutely defenceless, and at the mercy of the world. Of course one may reason, it is inconceivable that any true man would do this; Possibly so; but it is equally not understandable that it should ever have been passed in the first instance; and still equally not understandable that it should have been permitted by the public to have remained law. I have asked pioneers when this law was passed and by whom; they reply: "Oh that was passed away back in old Sir John A's time. It is the same in Manitoba." Those may be the facts, I don't know; if they are, and the Dominion Government did originate it, the situation suggests that white men must have been marrying squaws so extensively that Parliament deemed it a duty to make their white brothers real big chiefs. Whatever wisdom was behind the passing of the act in the first place it is without wisdom as applied to the present condition, and surely repugnant to any decent-minded persons. And if the bachelors of Saskatchewan do not disturb themselves and have this law repealed, they deserve to be boycotted by worthy women. It is about time that the Indian spirit of the West or any other party of Canada was eradicated from our white civilization.

Saskatchewan   BEACON

HOME LOVING HEARTS, *Free Press Prairie Farmer*
January 7, 1914

CHILDREN GIVEN AWAY

Dear Miss Laurie—

I have been a silent reader of your page for nearly a year and like it fine.

Dear Miss Laurie, I have come for help, I am only sixteen years old and am adopted. I have a lovely home.

My father left my mother with three children, and of course, it was in Canada, and you know how hard it is to get work there, so my mother had to give us away, my brother was about 7 then, I was 4 years 5 months, my sister 4 months old.

My sister got a good home, a woman by the name of Mrs. Corbert got her, she is raising her as her own, because we don't know where she is.

Some people got my brother and they abused him, the last letter or word we received about him he was in the home. I don't know what home. Is there any near Winnipeg, as this is where we lived.

Now Miss Laurie if you could help me find my brother, or any of the members, I would be grateful to you. He will be about 19 years old now. His name is Willie Cooper.

My mother is married again. She has a good husband now, her first one drank, that's why he left her. He loved drink more than us. My foster mother and father want me always to write to my mother, which I do.

Miss Laurie I do so hope the women of Canada get the vote, they have the vote here in Idaho, we also have prohibition here, which is certainly a blessing. I suppose you have snow there, we have just beautiful weather here. Well Miss Laurie if you don't think this is worth printing I won't be offended, but will write and tell you about beautiful Idaho. Will some of the members please write me as my address is with Miss Laurie. Will close with a recipe for a chocolate cake I took first prize on. I will sign my pen name

SWEET IDAHO

MOTHERS' LETTERS, *Grain Growers' Guide*
April 1, 1914

METHODS IN CHILD RAISING

Dear Miss Beynon:

My own children have grown up and I am now mothering two wee girlies who lost their dear father in 1912, so I have had to call to mind many lessons learnt in years gone by.

To young mothers I would say, "Have a fixed time for everything in your baby's life."

I know it may be difficult at first, but it will pay you in the end. The reason so many babies cry is because their little stomachs are over loaded, causing pain and discomfort.

If for any reason you are unable to nurse your baby, try barley water and new milk. Take two teaspoons of pearl barley, wash well and then simmer in a pint of water until half the water has boiled away. Strain, and add an equal quantity of new milk, and be sure your bottle is clean. Never make more than the above quantity at a time, for the barley soon sours. This is a splendid food for children of all ages.

I have found out that when a baby cries, sometimes they are thirsty. Boil some water and, when cold, sweeten slightly and give it in a feeding bottle or out of a cup. Never rock your baby to sleep. Lay him down awake and leave him. Have a regular time for bed and never take him up for strangers.

A mother must deny herself many things, but will it not be worth while when she sees her children grow strong and well and a pleasure instead of a burden? I suppose I am old-fashioned but I do not think children should be allowed to listen to conversations between elders on business, etc. Their young minds often receive wrong impressions. To my mind children of today are far too old in their ways. Let them have their child life to the full. The cares and work of the world will come soon enough and childhood's days should be the sweetest and brightest of all.

GRANDMOTHER

MOTHERS' LETTERS, *Grain Growers' Guide*
April 1, 1914

HEALTH AND MORALITY

This department should be highly valued by every woman who is a reader of The Grain Growers' Guide. It gives us the privilege of discussing freely experiences which may be helpful to all. Yet how often we meet those who deem it immodest to speak or write on subjects which are of vital importance.

We frequently hear of the little boy requiring to be circumcised, but how many mothers know that occasionally little girls require similar treatment.

When my little girl was a year old I noticed a strong tendency on the part of the child to relieve some irritation—even after the bath. I became alarmed lest one so young should be forming unchaste habits. Upon investigation I discovered something unnatural and made no delay in consulting our doctor. A slight operation was performed and with a little extra care for a few weeks the trouble was eliminated.

While conversing with the doctor he said, "Such cases are exceptional, but I believe many little girls are neglected, which causes them to form immoral habits."

Our children may form immoral habits without being in companionship with the rude and vulgar. It may be uncleanliness or it may be some form of disease which lays the foundation of what may in later years shipwreck our child. Is it not, therefore, our duty to take care that there is no physical defect and to insist on perfect cleanliness? Then by careful watchfulness and helpful counsel lead our little ones to pure noble manhood and womanhood.

A MOTHER

Plate 14. E. Cora Hind, commercial and agricultural columnist, *Free Press Prairie Farmer* (1901-1930), no date (E. Cora Hind Coll. 1, Harry Steele, photographer, Provincial Archives of Manitoba [N 978]).

Plate 15. Workers at the original Pacific Milk Plant Creamery, 1909 (Delta Museum and Archives, Delta, British Columbia [1980-52-59]).

Plate 16. Bread and jam, 1916 (Jessop Coll. 33, Provincial Archives of Manitoba [N 4026]).

Plate 17. Tennis at the William Law farm, Roblin, Manitoba, circa 1915 (Sport-Tennis Coll. 1, Provincial Archives of Manitoba [N 9878]).

Plate 18. At the lake, circa 1900 (Virden Coll. 32, Provincial Archives of Manitoba [N 17637]).

Plate 19. Volunteers for King and Country. Leona Whitworth in the garden with her father Isaac and brother Fred, circa 1915 (Delta Museum and Archives, Delta, British Columbia [1970-1-712]).

HOME LOVING HEARTS, *Free Press Prairie Farmer*
April 12, 1914

WHAT DO YOU THINK?

Dear Lillian Laurie,

Can you spare me space to express my views on the woman question, or rather I think I should say the family question?

I have noticed that many women say, "Woman's place is in the home." Now, what I would like to know is:

"Who said woman's place is home?"

"If woman's place is the home, then shouldn't every woman have a home?"

Then there are women who say, "Politics is man's business!"

Now, I would like to know who knows what is man's business and what is woman's business!

Now to deal with the first question, "Woman's place is the home."

I am a woman, a wife and a mother. I have four children, and I was left to care for those children when the oldest was eight years old. I had not been trained to do any kind of work except housework. I believed that "woman's place is in the home," but when I couldn't pay my rent, my home was taken from me. I wanted a home badly enough, and I wanted to be in it, but the landlord didn't see it that way. He thought my place was outside of the home if I couldn't pay to stay in, and I got out.

I tried to get work, but the only kind of housework I could get was charring. All who wanted help wanted a woman or girl who would stay in the house, and they could not take me in with my children. Charring means going into people's houses and doing their hardest and dirtiest work. I did it for awhile, but it left me so tired and worn out that I could not care for my children. It may be womanly work. It may be the proper thing for a woman to do, but I don't think it is. I don't think a woman because she is a woman should have to do the dirty menial work of the world and wear herself out until she is not fit to care for her children or to enjoy life at all.

I began to revolt against my condition. My children were being neglected. I was tired and weary and discouraged all the time. I spent my time doing everybody's dirty work, and getting less for it than people who did nice easy work and worked shorter hours. I saw women in business offices with no more brains than I had earning a good living, but they were doing what some people call "man's work."

Now I would like to know why people call certain work men's work, and other work, women's work.

I started out to find something else to do, and in my search I found more men than women cooking. I found men waiting on tables, I found men doing the washing in laundries, I found men making both men's and women's clothes, I found men trimming women's hats, I found men doing housework—in fact, I found men doing practically all the work that some people call "women's work."

I found men taking the work from women, and the women taking what was left, generally the hardest and the dirtiest. So I said to myself, "There is no such thing as "man's work," or "woman's work." There is the work of the world, and the one who can do any of the work best, should do it, be they men or women.

With this idea in mind I started out to find something to do. I did not care in the least whether it was what is called woman's work or whether it was man's work. I had a family to support and I was going to do my best to support them, and I didn't care a straw whether people thought I was womanly or not. When you see want staring your family in the face, you don't hesitate about what people will say.

There was just one thing I understood thoroughly, and that was roadmaking. My father had contracted for clearing land, making roads and grading for railroads. I had been with him a great deal and I had kept his accounts. I did it in a rough, crude way that I could understand, but that would not have suited anyone else. Father had failed, because of contracting too low, for a big job, and he died soon after. My mother soon followed him and there was nothing left for me.

I thought about it for a long time, and finally decided to try my father's business. I got an old friend to advance me the necessary money to begin, and to help me get a small contract for making a road. I was very nervous at first, but I made fairly well, and I soon got another.

It is not necessary to tell all my ups and downs. I made money from the first, and now I am what is called well fixed. My children are well educated. I have a comfortable home and enough to help anyone in need. It is true that I have had to do what is called man's work. I have put on overalls and a smock and worked. But never once was I as tired as after a day of charring. And I find that now I have made good people don't seem to think I was unwomanly.

WORKER

SCHOOL PROBLEMS

Dear Editor:

It has been with considerable amusement that I, with several other teachers, have been following the various controversies in your interesting column. First was the English versus German letters, and of course, we all cheered for Betsy. I have been in foreign settlements and teaching in foreign schools and I say "Amen, Betsy." But by far the most interesting and laughable is Thistleseed's trouble.

Poor "Experienced Teacher" surely brought an avalanche on her head that time.

You know, in enumerating the chores she does Thistleseed mentions a furnace and a great deal of stock. Does it sound as though they were too poverty stricken to send their children to school both winter and summer? They probably have a car, too. She seems to be laboring under the delusion that no one but the teacher receives any benefit from the school. They must have been unfortunate in their choice of teachers. Do your children learn nothing, Thistleseed? Are they subnormal?

Now, listen. I too am an experienced teacher, and am on my second year in a Ruthenian district. This is the third school which has become a yearly school instead of a summer school in my hands. And not one has regretted it. Of course there were kicks; no reform ever was put across without kicks. But the parents of the children were surprised at the extra progress their children have made. You see when you keep them at home all winter they forget all they learned. Also, during hot days in summer the children learn practically nothing. Any teacher of any experience will bear me out in that.

As to the children coming to a cold school, she is dreaming. I live in a small house on the school ground, and I had a rousing fire at 8 o'clock every morning. And it happens that "Experienced Teacher" did the same. Also, both in my school and that of "Experienced Teacher," the children have a hot lunch at noon. Now, what do you say, Thistleseed?

Also for two years I taught a school of 52 pupils, did the sewing, cooking, washing and baking for three adults and two children, drove 3-1/2 miles to school and built my own fires when I got there.

It was the first I realized how overpaid and underworked we teachers are, and I thank Thistleseed. "Live and Learn."

RESIDENTIAL TEACHER

PRIM ROSE AT HOME, *Family Herald and Weekly Star*
November 18, 1914

A "BACHER'S" WIFE

Dear Prim Rose:

I wonder what "Singlestick" would think of a wife having to start all the fires in the morning, summer and winter, get the breakfast ready and then call her "Willie" to eat it. I do all the chores, feed from twelve to fifteen hogs, milk seven to twelve cows the year around, cut nearly all the wood, carry it in and fill the water pail. I have to work in the harvest and hay field as long as there is anything to do—and I also do all the stacking. If "Single stick" would come out here I would show him what work is and how some women have to work, and the thanks they get for all they do. I am not allowed to have five cents to spend.

I came out west ten years ago and have been married eight years. I have not had a happy day since the first year of my marriage. My husband had bached for twenty-three years and I am only allowed to think as he does. I was a widow with one child, and that child is all my happiness. I don't know what I should do without her. She is sixteen now. People ask me why I do not leave him but I promised to take him for better or worse, and I got the worst. I promised to live with him till death parted us and I shall do as I promised the Lord, no matter how miserable my life may be. It will be a grand thing when women get the vote.

Alberta   A BROKEN-HEARTED WIFE

PRIM ROSE AT HOME, *Family Herald and Weekly Star*
March 24, 1915

A VOICE FROM VANCOUVER

Dear Prim Rose:

Those who have read Girls' Friend's letter in your issue of May 3rd will see that she has a good grasp of the present situation between bachelors and spinsters, and has given the best advice on the subject. I thank her much for joining our club and I am sure all girls and bachelors will welcome her letters. She does not think any of them would homestead a ranch if they knew the expense, hardship, loneliness, etc. If spinsters and girls will carefully figure out Intruder's letter of the same issue, they will form a good idea of what it means to clear 20 acres of B.C. bush land. $300 an acre is an average price for a lot of it, and they can calculate $200 an acre on clearing heavy bush. Intruder took three years to clear 10 acres, but those having the ready cash and who want land cleared quickly will do better to employ a large logging engine, use powder, and employ a man experienced in blasting and cable clearing. Kindly forward the two cards enclosed to Wrathy Spinster. They will give her an idea of what she will have to clear in B.C. to make a home.

Vancouver, British Columbia   BROTHER BACHELOR

———————

THE COUNTRY HOMEMAKERS, *Grain Growers' Guide*
April 29, 1915

WOMEN NEED TO GET OUT

Dear Miss Beynon:

I have intended writing to you ever since I came home from the Regina Convention. I am so glad to have met you there. I can feel now that we are indeed friends. Your page in the *Guide*, is what I always look forward to, and in reading your editorial of March 10, "Whose business is it?" I decided to write at once as you wrote on a question that I am greatly interested in, as I know from experience the lonely life of the pioneer's wife on the prairies. When I came on to our homestead nine years ago with my husband and baby girl one year old, there were very few women who could speak the English language. We were 60 miles from the end of the railroad and twenty-five miles from the nearest doctor. But we decided to make the best of it and altho our house was only fifteen feet by fifteen feet, it was home to us. We also made room for a homeless young man who had his leg broken and could not manage for himself. Often it was three months at a time that I did not see the face of a woman, but I was not unhappy. We had a number of bachelor neighbors and we invited them for dinners and evening parties and did all we could to make life a little pleasanter for them, and thus we found happiness in giving a little pleasure to others.

We lived on the homestead there for five years. In that time two more babies came to our house with no other medical attention than that given by an inexperienced neighbor woman.

Then we moved to another farm nearer to town. I had become so used to not going any place that I never thought of doing so, just stopped at home and kept at everlasting work, which never seemed to get less, until with overwork and the eternal monotony my health gave way and I was a complete wreck. Then I began to realize how narrow the last two years of my life had been since moving from the homestead. I did not know my neighbor women who only lived two miles from me, and how I wished in my illness for a kind friend. I did not blame my neighbors as I knew I was as much to blame as they and that we were all making a big mistake. In looking through the Grain Grower' Guide I read where the women of Saskatchewan were forming a W.G.G.A. I was quite taken with the idea and thought that we should do likewise. I asked my husband to go with me to the home of a neighbor, whom I had never seen. The result was that we now have a Women's Section of the G.G.A. with twenty-five paid up members. Some will say, "But I have not the time for such things." To such I will say, "Make time. You can do it, if you only think so." When your work gets on your nerves get out and away and if that is not possible, go out in the bluffs and listen to the birds singing. If your lot is a hard one, don't sit around and cry about it, get busy and do something. Smile and others will smile with you.

I find my work does not suffer when I take half a day off to attend our meeting or visit a neighbor, and whereas my doctor's bills used to be from fifty to one hundred dollars per year, in the last year since I have taken up other interests outside my home, I have not had one dollar of a doctor's fee. I might say my worst troubles were bad nerves and a weak heart.

But I think the best time of all was the Regina Convention, the first time for me to go away and leave my husband and the children at home alone, but they managed nicely and I enjoyed my trip so very much. It is something to think about with pleasure while attending my home duties and perhaps help to lighten the life of others by my telling them about it. I can understand the hopeless feeling of the women whom you write about, as I have often felt the same as they, and thought at times that life was not worth living but I did not write and tell anyone of my feelings at that time. I consider we are disloyal to our husbands when we do so, as in almost every case our homes are the very best they can afford to give us. Then why make life hard for them by our discontent and thus make our home miserable for all?

I will not ask you to publish this long letter, Miss Beynon, but if there are some parts of it that you think may be of interest to others you can publish them and I would be pleased to write anyone if they care to write to me. With kindest regards to you, Miss Beynon, and all home-makers and G.G.A. members, I will sign myself

HOPE

THE COUNTRY HOMEMAKERS, *Grain Growers' Guide*
March 17, 1915

WHO'LL HELP THIS BABY?

There is in Winnipeg, a poor scrawny little boy of three years who can scarcely walk because he is so badly nourished. His family have had such difficulty in supplying their large family with food and clothing that the wee laddie has gone hungry and more often still been fed with stuff that gave little nourishment to his small body. Some friends of his have asked if I could find some people in the country who would be willing to take this poor delicate little chap and feed him up well for a few months. Unfortunately, in one sense, his parents are unwilling to part with him permanently, so that it would have to be purely a labor of love. But if there is anyone willing to undertake this charge for the sake of helping a needy family at this time of stress, I wish they would communicate with me.

FRANCIS MARION BEYNON

THE COUNTRY HOMEMAKERS, *Grain Growers' Guide*
April 21, 1915

MANY HOMES FOR BABY

So many homes were found for the wee sick laddie all over Western Canada that we are giving notice here that he is being sent out in a few days to a farm not far distant from Winnipeg. Most cordially thanking our readers for their generous response to this appeal. —F.M.B.

THE COUNTRY HOMEMAKERS, *The Grain Growers' Guide*
April 12, 1915

FOUR LEAN YEARS IN FIVE

Dear Madam:

In reply to a letter by "Canadian" in your issue of February 17 asking how people can become so completely destitute of clothing in one year, I would like to say that the destitute districts are not suffering from one year's drought alone, but from four years of drought.

These people mostly homesteaded in 1909 or 1910 with enough capital to carry them for one and a half years. In the five succeeding years, owing to the drought, there has only been one paying crop, two years of total crop failure, and two in which the crop yielded about ten bushels to the acre of poor grade wheat. The year of the good crop, No.1 wheat only sold for 60 cents a bushel.

Living between twenty-five and a hundred miles from a town, all buying and selling has been carried on at a great disadvantage to the farmer, his freighting expenses have been enormous. So you will see that not in one year out of five has he been able to spare any cash for replenishing the wardrobe for himself or his family. I think your correspondent will agree, that old clothes which have been patched, mended and made over for four years, will have to be thrown away at last.

This is why the homesteaders are so terribly hard up for clothing this winter.

A HOMESTEADER'S WIFE

PRIM ROSE AT HOME, *Family Herald and Weekly Star*
December 1, 1915

VALUABLE FUR

Dear Prim Rose:

I don't see many letters from this part of Canada, so I thought, I would write. I am a trapper's wife and have lived up here for nine years. In winter my husband often comes home with martens and fishers, whose fur, you all know, is very valuable. In summer he fishes. There are seven canneries in the Inlet. Indian women do the canning, but there are some white women working there too.

For game we have bear, mountain goat and deer; the last are very plentiful.

I pass my time in the winter doing fancy work and reading. I have my little boy for a companion while my husband is away in the woods.

British Columbia   ALOHA TWIN

―――――――

HOME LOVING HEARTS, *Free Press Prairie Farmer*
December 15, 1915

Dear Lillian Laurie:

Having read the H.L.H.page for a long time now I thought I would like to write. I am a young mother with four little children. We live on a homestead, a nice and healthy place, but very few neighbors. How many mothers have experienced the loss of a good husband and father in this terrible war. My husband, who was an English reservist, was called to serve his country in August 1914. He has been in several battles in Belgium and France, and last month he returned home without a scratch. Do you not think it was wonderful? Of course, he was not the only one, but one of the lucky ones. But it was a terrible wrench to have him away, as only a wife who thinks anything at all of her husband knows. My baby was born in October, and had not seen his dad. What a reunion that was. Miss Laurie, only those who have experienced it know. Enough about myself. I am not by myself by a long way, I know.

I really think it is a shame to serve those poor soldiers as they did. Poor, sick and wounded without enough clothes to keep them warm after they had been fighting for us at home, doing their best for Canada, but I hope things like that will soon be seen to. My husband had lots of warm clothes, and his passage paid right home. His discharge was made out in England. Why should they be so different?

Concerning the two articles in our page this week, referring to the two murders. I pity that poor woman with all my heart, for I feel that she was quite justified in doing what she did. I am sure I should have done the same thing myself on impulse of the moment, if my husband had brought another woman in my house and taunted me. I would certainly sign today for that woman's release. Why should they make an exception of the man and make the woman suffer, for both are just the some if looked into. You may not all agree with me, but everybody has a right to think as she likes and this is just what I think.

I have homesteaded myself since my husband's absence, with my poor little ones. I have been doing the work my husband would have done, and hard work at that. Those that homestead and have crops to put in, know that it is not easy, but it had to be done, and nobody else to do it. My oldest son is only 6 years old, so he could not help. Well, I shall have to quit this time, or this may be too long to fill the corner of the page. So I will sign myself

AN ENGLISH SOLDIER'S WIFE

If Allie has not disposed of the fur coat and boots I would willingly pay postage. My address is with the editor.

PRIM ROSE AT HOME, *Family Herald and Weekly Star*
January 5, 1916

A PITIFUL HEART

Dear Prim Rose:

With regard to the collecting of insects I wondered if there couldn't be a better way to destroy them other than pinning them on a pad. I think everything of that kind should be done in a way that would prevent all unnecessary suffering.

The same thing also applies to the trapping of animals; as sometimes they may have to stay in the traps for days before being released and I think it ought to be arranged that the traps should be visited more often.

I have thought the traps might be lined with something or made so as to cause as little pain as possible. It makes one feel that they would not care to wear furs procured at such a price.

FARMER

Doubtless a letter addressed to the Natural History Club of this paper would bring you helpful advice in reply. You did not send in your name and address.—Prim Rose.

PRIM ROSE AT HOME, *Family Herald and Weekly Star*
January 26, 1916

WHEN A MAN ENLISTS

Dear Prim Rose:

The great rolling prairie is very fascinating, but in the part of Alberta where I live, trees, which are lovely, are very scarce, but I like the country very much.

I feel called upon by "Tipperary's" letter to say a few words in defence of the "healthy young wife who is quite able to look after herself and children" letting her husband join the colors. Of course there are some wives who would be left with plenty of this world's goods, but what about the numberless wives who would be left with very little or nothing? Employment is very hard to get at present and there would be the little children to be cared for.

As to the aged parents, there are homes built on purpose for such as are unable to keep themselves, and those who are able could pay some kind women to live with them and care for them. So in both cases the aged parents could spare their only son for war.

I am "a healthy young wife," with three small children two of whom are under two years of age. My only trade is housekeeping and I feel that I would have a very hard battle, securing employment and taking care of these wee tots too. I don't see how I can spare my husband for the war. I would like to have other people's opinions on this subject.

Alberta   EVANGELINE

The Government and the Patriotic Fund care for the wife and children when a man enlists, and contributes to the support of parents, too, in some cases. —*Prim Rose.*

HOME LOVING HEARTS, *Free Press Prairie Farmer*
January 26, 1916

CAN'T ALTER CIRCUMSTANCES

Dear Editor and Members:

Some weeks ago a note from the editor regarding a prairie woman who felt old at 40 with 13 children aroused my indignation. Thirteen children! Suffering humanity! No wonder she feels old, bitter and resentful. Yes, there is just one kind of people who makes us more weary that the ones who sit down and get sorry for themselves. The ones who have no heart or sympathy for anyone but themselves. L.L. says: "If we are free-will beings we must make things go our way." Then in the next breath, "The woman with thirteen children has not much chance." This coming from one who has not one child and knows nothing of what the drudgery of homework means, to say nothing of the naggings of one, two, four, thirteen children.

How is "free will" going to exonerate a women who cares for a life with any degree of comfort, leisure, pleasure, usefulness or peace from the drudgery, disorder, poverty, loneliness and contention of a cheerless prairie home of a large family.

If a woman marries a man and settles down on a prairie farm (as a number of them must do in order to keep the women in the city living in comfort) she is not responsible for the number of children that come. The children being here, crops having failed, finances not increasing beyond daily necessities, help cannot be afforded. Then who must do the housework, outside chores, milking, tending babies, sweeping, dusting, washing, cooking, churning, sewing, etc., etc., etc. It must all be managed by the mother and she struggles cheerfully or wearily on according to her temperament, but whichever way she may feel about it she has the same tasks to perform, the same heavy burdens to meet day by day, the same monotonous round to tread day by day, year by year, varied only by the added care of a new baby each year, and the only lull the mother gets in her dogged treadmill, is the few days' rest she gets in bed when the young stranger comes which are thoroughly necessary to fortify her for the extra pile of work that will be found awaiting her after her few days absence from the field of action. The city woman would hold up her hands in horror at the thought of not having a nurse, doctor, and housemaid at this time, but the prairie woman is fortunate indeed if she can have a doctor, and the yearly visit from the doctor is in many cases the only intellectual person the mother ever meets in her secluded life.

My husband and I often laugh and chat after it is all over, about the deplorable state the household gets in while I am confined to my room. The sight of it, and unkempt children, nearly make me faint when he carries me downstairs. Then while in a decidedly convalescent state house-cleaning must be done, loads of washing, baking, ironing and heaps of other neglected work must be mastered. This would not mean so much if one could go leisurely on with some little diversion occasionally to cheer one, but I am considered an excellent manager and I find that I must rise by five in the morning and prepare a decidedly hasty toilet and rush like mad to have breakfast on time. After breakfast it takes a stout heart and strong nerve to tackle the burden of dishwashing, separator, milk things, disorderly house, interspersed with quarrels, naggings, and interruptions of the children, and yet if I could be free from the distracting naggings of the children I would work my finger nails off with pleasure. But the tired mother never gets one hour's cessation from it all and the most eloquent poet could not paint with his pen the torture the nerve-aching mothers endure. Trench life is colorless in comparison.

I find that without one hour's cessation I must rush with a capital "R" from five in the morning till ten and often eleven at night. I run from one task to another. I do only the necessary tasks to live in any semblance of a refined life. The children shoulder their own share of life's struggle, and they are exceedingly well-trained. But I am considered a modern woman, one who is keeping pace with the times. I always manage to keep one dress (made by myself) hanging in the wardrobe that has a semblance of up-to-dateness about it. I go to the Ladies' Institute once a month. Hubby and I take turns in going to Sunday school with the children, and when I have energy enough to push my end of the work a little harder I ask a few of the most congenial people of the district in.

Often one big rocking chair holds Hubby and I and all the children, and we have a jolly household. We are in extreme poverty, but our meals from farm produce daintily cooked and served a king might envy.

The carpets are threadbare, the furniture is screaming with cheapness, and when I give way to my desire for beautiful furniture it stabs me to the soul. I detest farm life. I long for the city and society and other lines of work. I am a refined woman and menial labor is obnoxious to me, but I do not sit down and deplore my lot, but I am a fair example of a prairie woman and shoulder my lot with flinty determination, and unwavering courage.

Three years ago I visited Lillian Laurie in her home. I compared my own dank, wet, soggy steps as I walked up her beautiful, clean, gray, painted ones. The door was answered by a servant, who ushered me into Miss. L's study where she was waiting in comfort and luxury. The touch of a bell brought the servant to render any little necessary service. Contrast the two lives of prairie and city women. If perchance we have a moment to pick up a paper we may notice glowing accounts of L.L.'s and other women giving eloquent addresses to large audiences. Many a prairie women is quite as well able to, but such things are for her as unobtainable as the moon.

Well, we don't mind shouldering our lot if we have to. Some must live in the country, but while we bear the brunt of the battle to keep the city woman in comfort and luxury, we do deplore being told that "If we are not getting what we ought to out of life we are responsible for that fact."

We are not master of circumstances, and though amid all our struggles we may remain unscathed by the city sister's criticism, we cannot extricate ourselves from the home of a large family, or its treadmill of duties, so our dear sisters of the prairie.

"Let us then be up and doing
   With a heart for any fate,
   Still achieving, still pursuing,
   Learn to labor and to wait.

I do not expect my letter will be published. However, the only outlet we get for our ideas is on paper, and I had to remain up late after the others were in bed to write this.

A Happy New Year to the editor and all the members,

DETERMINATION

HOME LOVING HEARTS, *Free Press Prairie Farmer*
March 21, 1916

THE QUESTION OF POPULATION

Dear Miss Laurie,

I have been an interested reader of your page for some time. People say save the children! Now, I have often thought it would be a good idea to tax the bachelors, so as to encourage them to marry. Then as each child was born lighten the tax. Then after, say, four take off the tax, and after that number the government pay so much for each child to help raise them up to a certain age. I know so many people who have just one child and are having too good a time to have any more, and some people have three or four say they can't afford to keep any more. Now I think those who have no more for the sake of having a good time should be taxed heavily, and those that can't have children of their own should adopt them and be taxed accordingly, as if they had them of their own. There are so many getting killed off in this dreadful war the British will soon be run out, and the Germans keep having all they can, so they will be sure to win the next war. I have often watched and wondered why someone did not write on this subject. Now, Miss Laurie, if you don't think fit to print this in your wonderful page I wish you would write and tell me your idea about it. I am such a poor hand at writing and spelling. I hope if you do print this you will kindly correct mistakes.

Thanking you, Dear Miss Laurie, for your trouble,

SASKATCHEWAN ROSE

PRIM ROSE AT HOME, *Family Herald and Weekly Star*
August 2, 1916

Dear Prim Rose:

Before I married I taught six years in Alberta and British Columbia. Now I am classed among the "blessed," and must admit that we are a happy family. My little girl of three years is a finish to our home comforts.

We live in the famous Okanagan Valley, and the "land of the big red apples." We have a private residence, three horses, a cow, a calf, a colt; also a splendid vegetable and fruit garden. So home is truly an ideal spot.

Vernon, a short distance away, has a camp of some 15,000 soldiers. Many ride over on Sundays and holidays in autos to see the camp. They are the 172nd, the 131st, and the 54th and Western Irish Battalions; the camp is a fine sight to behold.

"Jack the Trapper" desired information about Vancouver. I have visited the city frequently and my parents' home is in New Westminster. The chief industries of Vancouver are lumber-milling, shipping, exporting, also canneries—(fruit and vegetable), fishing and fruit farming.

There is a lovely natural park, the third largest in the world, I believe.

Residences, especially in Fairview and Shaughnessy Heights, are lovely. Magnificent stores, tramways and all manner of other traffic make it a gay city. I hope that this short description will help "Jack."

Will any soldier from Canada, England, or any other of the countries of the Allies please write to me.

British Columbia   A LOVING WIFE

OUR WELFARE PAGE, *Saturday Press and Prairie Farm*
August 19, 1916

WAKE UP! FARM WOMEN

Dear Mrs. V. McNaughton:

As a woman of "no occupation," I naturally have a great deal of leisure. To show that I have, I have enumerated a few of the things I do: (I have four children, the oldest nine). I cook, milk, make butter, raise chickens, garden, sew, wash and iron, and keep a six-room house, with no help. In winter, when my children couldn't go to school, I taught them and they were ahead of their classes when spring came, yet I have "no occupation." Before I married, I worked in an office from eight o'clock to six. After that, I worked or played as I pleased, yet I had an "occupation." Now, I work from any hour in the morning to any hour at night and I am never through. Are we farmer's wives always to be "dumb driven cattle" in the eyes of the government? It's time we were up and showing them a few things; and that we can do by means of the vote. I suppose most women have found that we still have no voice in school or municipal matters unless we pay taxes in our own name. How many of us do? Not enough, I fear, to make much difference in school or municipal elections.

There is another matter I should like to mention. What in the world are mothers thinking of that they make soldiers of their boys from the time they are babies? I refer to the uniforms being sold for boys of all ages. Wherever I go I see small boys wearing them.

Now, I very firmly believe in teaching children to be good citizens, to love their country and to be loyal to it: but I do not believe that a military uniform has any place in such teaching. They are only learning to love the uniform. Are we mothers to go on and teach our boys to love war instead of peace? Do we see our children now infants, as soldiers of the future and engaged in another awful carnage such as we have at present? It seems inconceivable that women should go on making soldiers of their children, instead of teaching them to hate war. We have in our power to help make the future and war should have no place in that future; but we must do it through our children.

NO OCCUPATION

HOME LOVING HEARTS, *Free Press Prairie Farmer*
October 4, 1916

THE GRANDMOTHER SPEAKS

Dear Home Loving Hearts:

I really don't suppose I would have written to your club if I had not picked up the Free Press at a friend's house that I was visiting here in Alberta and saw "Try Again's" letter.

I extend my sympathy to that girl "Try Again" mentions, and I do not blame her in the least. But are all heroes like that one she speaks of? I think not all, but, unfortunately the majority of them are. Does no one think that a boy who leads a girl astray has a mother and what she thinks? I suppose the mother of those heroes do not count, but dear readers, they do, more than you think. I know, as I myself am the grandmother of a war baby!

My son enlisted in one of the first battalions that left Canada to partake in the great struggle, and, as he is our only child, naturally his father and I think a lot of him.

But to get back to what I want to tell. It was on Christmas eve, and our son was home for a few short days on leave, and he and I were sitting in front of a leaping fire in our cozy living room, my husband having gone to see a neighbor nearby. We had no lamp and the room was quiet, save for the crackle of the spruce logs on the hearth, and I sat back in my chair and watched my silent son, wondering. He seemed absent-minded and troubled, and I was sure he had something to tell me, as he had.

"Mother," he said, slowly slipping over onto the arm of my chair, "I have something to tell you—something that isn't pleasant, but you are the only one I can tell it to." And sitting there, his fingers crumpling my collar, he told me how, shortly after he had enlisted, he had met a girl, a clerk in a nearby town, and what had happened one fine moonlit night after a drive. "I don't think she knew what she was doing," he continued hurriedly. "I don't suppose I did either for that matter; but I am awfully sorry now when it is too late. Most of the fellows wouldn't think twice about it, and let her bear the brunt of the whole thing, but somehow I just can't. She has no relatives or nothing. I'm sorry, mother, I've made such a mess of everything, but can't I help her somehow?"

I must say the confession had left me strangely sick and numb, but I rallied myself against the shock the best I could, and turning so I could look my son straight in the eyes, I said quietly, though the effort cost me a lot more that I cared to admit:

"Son, the only honorable way to make up to this girl you have so wronged is to marry her."

I don't think he quite expected that, for I saw him wince, but he is a soldier every inch of him, and as he rose he said gravely:

"Yes, I suppose that's the only way. Good night, mother and God bless you." And he marched away off to his room, where I heard him pacing the floor long after midnight. I believe I loved my boy more that night than I ever did before. The blow he had dealt me was a hard and a bitter one, but he was at least sorry for the disgrace he had brought upon an innocent girl and anxious to make amends at the expense of his own freedom, and I loved him for it.

As he went back to his own regiment, he was married to this girl, and I was waiting at the station in the car to meet her as she got off the train.

I expected a different kind of girl than the one I met, and I was a little surprised when I saw her. She was small and slim, with large dark eyes that had a diffident look in them as they met mine as I took her small gloved hand. She was neatly and well dressed, although her clothes had seen much wear, and as I tucked her into the car I felt she could have been much worse and I could almost feel a load lifted off my heart.

On the way home she said little, her big, mournful eyes on the white road ahead, her thin white face steady and unflinching, her whole attitude that of defiance, and any kind of confidential approach was instantly put off.

The three weeks following her arrival gave me much food for thought. She was quiet and unapproachable, but willing to help, and I wondered helplessly what I could do to make her see that I felt no bitterness toward her, and that I wanted to love her as I did my son, till one day I found her curled up on the couch in a limp heap, her whole body racking with big tearless sobs. I sat down and put my arms around that slender heap and as her sobs subsided she buried her face in my lap and murmured tearfully, "I did not know; I did not know. Mother never told me!" So there it was—"Mother never told me." Little by little it came out. How sure she was that I hated her, but tried be nice to her for my son's sake. How she had suffered for fear of the future, and how dreadfully ignorant she was of the opposite sex as well as her own. We had a long confidential talk there and then, and I won over my new daughter completely. In the weeks that followed when she was not poring over books with my husband, who fairly adored her, she was with me sewing on tiny garments as we talked about my son or the baby that was to come. As the months went by she grew better and her cheeks took on the rosy hue of health, as she took long walks out in the open air. She was such a sweet, gentle soul that the neighbors began to speak of her as "that nice little wife of your son." She read to sick people, she looked after children while their mothers were away and she enveloped you with cheer and goodwill like a blanket, and people forgot to give sarcastic hints and lift their eyebrows, as they had done the first few weeks when her name was mentioned, and I sent up a prayer of thankfulness.

Then one day, late in May, I sent my son a telegram saying that he had a big son and two days later he came breezing in where I was just rolling up the baby after the nurse had given it its bath. He had come so unexpectedly that he took me by surprise and I stared at him open mouthed.

"Say, I got special leave to come and see that son of mine," he broke in bluntly, advancing towards the bundle in my arms. Then, as I pushed back the blanket from the baby's face, "Shish! It looks like a tomato!" He was home a week. Then he left for his regiment, which shortly afterwards sailed for England, leaving his young son and wife at home.

The boy is nearly a year and a half old now, and when visitors come he shows them his daddy's picture—his daddy, who has received the V.C. and is now an officer, who sends him funny things from the front.

So you see, dear readers, there are soldiers who can be heroes in more ways than one, and I thank God that my boy has proven himself a man for his country's sake, as well as that of his son, who may also some day be a soldier. And I am very proud of my soldier son and my pretty gentle daughter, not to mention their curly headed boy.

THE MOTHER OF A SOLDIER

HOME LOVING HEARTS, *Free Press Prairie Farmer*
December 6, 1916

ADVICE FOR EXPECTANT MOTHERS

Dear Lillian Laurie,—

I just cannot keep my pen from paper any longer. I do think it is about as great a sin for a woman to write about Mother of Soldier's boys as R.B.S. wrote in Nov. 15 Free Press as it would be for those boys to do wrong to a girl. I know if I was that poor mother I would wish to get hold of her and I am much afraid if I did there would be a horse-whip in evidence. It is a terrible strain on we women that have boys at the front, when they may be wounded or dead even and us not know for weeks. I never get up in the morning without thinking I may get bad news today, and I know other mothers are the same. I have a teacher boarding with me and she is from a town where there are sixteen war babies and she says that both mothers and girls are a lot to blame for so many war babies. She can tell of plenty of cases of her schoolmates where the mothers never think anything of it if the girls are not in at 12 and pay no attention as to who they are with. Just a word to expectant mothers. I suffered just terribly with my first four and with my last two scarcely any in comparison, and what I did was as soon as I knew I was pregnant to take a good sponge bath all over every night. I also chewed the slippery elm bark and swallowed the juice. My own mother told me to use the bark, also my husband's mother, and I never would. And another lady here, who came almost dying with the first two, tried an Indian woman's remedy. That is, take a medium warm sitz bath to the waist line every night for one-half hour the last two months of pregnancy, and after drying rub the abdomen and the cords in the groin with glycerine or sweet oil, and she was sick just fifteen minutes, and as all three were boys it surely must have helped her. The doctors in the best hospital in Edmonton told her she could not give birth without instruments, and instead of lying in bed for weeks and being a weak wreck when she got up she felt as well as ever in her life in eight days, and declares she could have dressed her baby at the start. Now, dear Miss Laurie, print the remedy part, if all is not worth it, and I believe all the sane readers would be glad if you would drop such grouchy letters as R.B.S. wrote in the W.P.B. All success to you.

A SOLDIER'S MOTHER

OUR WELFARE PAGE, *The Saturday Press and Prairie Farm*
January 6, 1917

QUERY?

Dear Mrs. McNaughton: —

I am not long arrive in this country and what you call a foreigner. In your page I yet sometimes read, so will you please what I ask to me explain. In this country, Saskatchewan, Manitoba and Alberta, the people do for prohibition speak absolute. I am so told this is not so, it must not, cannot be, for why, because long, long time ago, some very wise men, they found out they themselves more than enough for that time know, so laws they make for everybody who after them live.

Now, Mrs. Editor, please tell me is this a joke on me or everybody, won't you? I as well hear that what you direct legislation call which is where I am come from, is all shut up in this same box. Please tell me what sort of joke is also this?

NEW COUNTRY-WOMAN

N.B.—Glad to have your letter. Will try to answer your questions next week.—V. McN.

HOME LOVING HEARTS, *Free Press Prairie Farmer*
January 10, 1917

ON MIDWIVES

Dear Lillian Laurie:

Re Dr. Thompson's letter as to the practice of midwifery in Saskatchewan. I have often wondered after reading the woman's page in the Free Press and Prairie Farmer that no one took up the question.

It gives me the heartache to read the helpless, hopeless letters at times seen there, re having babies on the prairies.

If I could write as I think and feel on the matter, I might interest some poor despondent, expectant mother. I do not know about the so-called midwives belonging to alien countries, but I do know that the training of the midwife in England is very thorough to take a normal care of childbirth, also to recognize at once if it is abnormal, also what the abnormality consists in.

As regards a registered practitioner, Dr. Thompson knows full well that the act of a normal parturition does not need a practitioner of medicine, as there is none needed, as kind Mother Nature supplies all necessaries in a case of normal confinement, which I expect amounts to about 95 per cent.

A very great percentage of the obstetrical work in the United Kingdom, is done by trained midwives, with marked success. A medical man informed me a few years ago that there was no percentage at all of deaths due to confinement in the United Kingdom.

After having a very large family myself, and seeing so much suffering and neglect caused by the untrained midwife, and my own experience, there seemed to me nothing so much worth while for me to do but train for obstetrical work, which I did very successfully, as I was wholehearted in the work, and was most successful in the same for a number of years, till my health began to fail, and I still have as great a desire to help and comfort the distressed and helpless mothers. But if I went and gave successful help, with knowledge and experience I have had, which has been very wide and varied, the law in Saskatchewan tells me that it would fine me $100. But a woman going to help without either knowledge or training there would not be any notice taken of the fact. The reason to me seems quite obvious.

I do think that a woman to assist successfully must have quite a considerable knowledge of the mechanism of parturition, also how to control severe hemorrhage, which can only be gained by good training, theory and experience, until she can get help if needed, and having the knowledge can always take a normal case, and if she can stay and nurse the patient through to convalescence would mean a great deal for the safety and comfort of both mother and child on the prairie, and the expense would not be much more that the doctor's one visit, and very often the child has been born a considerable time before the doctor arrives and often without anyone oversighting it at all. So much for the wonderful and beautiful methods of nature.

If there are any untoward symptoms supervene after confinement, they come about the third or fourth day, which really then needs both nursing skill and knowledge, which can only come through good training, both for normal delivery and nursing the care through intelligently, but the one thing that seems so undesirable, is that a young sensitive woman should be compelled to have a strange man thrust into the privacy of her bedroom, not as a matter of need or desire, but in the name of the law. Even the beast of the field will get away from their own kind, if possible, to be alone. Seems to me that the liberties of people are being exploited, for what?

I still hold three certificates gained from the training school and the Obstetrical society, London, England, and if I were only a few years younger, or could hope for a few more years of good health, would return to do the work again, as the trained maternity nurse has a standing second only to the physician, whom she considers her best friend when help is needed.

MATERNITY

PRIM ROSE AT HOME, *Family Herald and Weekly Star*
July 3, 1917

THE SENSIBLE AGE

Dear Prim Rose,

I find this page a very delightful and instructive one, and at times vastly amusing. Don't you think the following lines express the requirements of most Western bachelors including Shocks?

"Wanted a wife who can handle a broom,
To brush down the cobwebs and sweep up the room,
To made decent bread that a fellow can eat;

Not the horrid compound you everywhere meet;
Who knows how to fry, to broil, and to roast,
Make a good cup of tea and a platter of toast;
A woman who washes, cooks, irons and stitches,
And sews up the rips in a fellow's old breeches;
A common sense creature, but still with a mind
To teach, and to guide, exalted, refined,
A sort of angel and house maid combined."

I should like correspondents of the other sex between 35 and 40, if they live near town and own good farms and good houses, not shacks. I am a good cook and buttermaker, and am fond of poultry.

SASKATCHEWAN NANCY

HOME LOVING HEARTS, *Free Press Prairie Farmer*
January 2, 1918

BRAVE LITTLE GIRL

Dear Members,—

I have often thought of writing and I hope that this short letter will be welcome. I am only fifteen, but that doesn't matter, I hope. I am keeping house for my brothers and sisters. My mother died last winter. She used to be a member of the H.L.H.'S page. There are eight children all younger that myself, and I don't find much time for writing. I think Wa Bun's letter just fine, and I quite agree with her about working on Sunday and speaking ill of other people. That's one thing I do hate—to hear people calling their neighbors and friends down to the lowest degree. We are all human beings and one person has faults just as much as another. Well, it is winter again. Today is the first snowstorm we have had this fall. We are all threshed. But didn't have much grain this year.—I remain, a new member,

PRAIRIE MAID

HOME LOVING HEARTS, *Free Press Prairie Farmer*
January 2, 1918

ANOTHER TRAGEDY

Dear Editor,—

In reply to the letter signed "One of Us," I would like to say a few words. I do certainly feel grateful for the kind letters that I have received in answer to my letter in your paper. A Discouraged Woman, Maybe I am a little selfish and inclined to dwell too much on my own trouble and sickness, but God knows I wrote with the full intention of helping some other woman to stop before she gets in such bad shape as I am in. Since writing the last letter the kind neighbor I spoke of is dead. She has four little children, and was always so strong and well I can't realize she is dead, and her three days' old baby as well. They are getting on fine as far as money goes. Her husband put up a beautiful new barn this fall. It did not matter that his family still lived in the two-roomed log shack he built when they homesteaded here. As long as his horses and cattle are warm and dry what matter, if the log shack was cold and damp. He will build a house after a while. Now the poor women is in her grave he won't need to. There seems to be something terribly wrong on the prairie. A woman gives up her life for her child and it is all right, but if a man's best mare if sick, how quick he can get a veterinary in. How terrible to lose a mare worth 250 dollars! But there are lots of women now. As one man said to my husband the day of the funeral: "Do men ever stop to realize what it means for a woman to bear his children, give the best years of her life for him and them, and then be glad to die?" I think a man should be compelled to build a decent house and have a well near the house before he can take a wife on the farm. Also he should be compelled to have a doctor in times of confinement and not depend upon a neighbor at such a time. My trouble all comes from that cause, too little care and getting about too soon. Well, dear Editor, this is a long letter, but will you kindly print it. If it only helps one woman I shall be satisfied. Again thank the other members for their kindness and sympathy.

DISCOURAGED WOMAN

Home Loving Hearts, *Free Press Prairie Farmer*
January 9, 1918

Municipal Hospitals

Dear Editor:

I have long been an interested reader of your page, but I have never had the courage to write before. I have been thinking of doing so ever since last September, for when I was out cooking for our threshing outfit a bachelor neighbor (at whose place we were) when we were discussing the provincial election, I said to him that I agreed with one lady, who had written to the page saying she had voted as best she could, but was still far from satisfied. This gentleman said, "Oh, if those women who write letters to the Free Press had as many dishes to wash as you have they would not find time for such a lot of nonsense." And right there I said to myself, says I, "Someday I'll show you I can write a letter to the Free Press and wash a lot of dishes too."

I saw in your note to the members that you would like to hear from anyone who could tell of the benefits of a municipal hospital. I will try to do so to the best of my ability. We have one in our district. A number of municipalities joined together or united, I should say, and any rate payer or member of the family of a rate payer gets attendance free of charge. Of course one has their own doctor bill to pay, also medicine, and they are at liberty in a very serious case to call in or put on duty a special nurse. It certainly is a great boon to the farmers, and those who live a long distance from medical attendance; in fact, I often wonder how we did without such benefits so long. My son was in there a year ago. He was taken with a very severe case of double pneumonia. He had to have two operations, and was twice given up by the doctors, but with the skill of faithful nurses and the best of attendance he pulled through, and now is nearly as strong and healthy as ever. He was in the hospital for over four months, and it cost him just the doctor's bill and attendance of a special nurse. Now, I do not mean that we consider cost in a case of life or death, but we on the prairie cannot very well afford large hospital bills and nurses' fees. And I am just pointing out how much one may benefit by the united municipal hospitals, for I know for a positive fact we could not have pulled him through such a severe sickness in our own small home. In our own municipality, in case of confinement, a woman's board is paid for two weeks in town previous to entering the hospital, so that they may not take a chance in staying away too long on account of being too poor to pay their board. Of course there are a number of improvements that could be made in it, but they are going to build a new hospital soon with all modern equipments. The taxes, as far as I understand, are at present about one dollar and seventy-five cents per quarter section extra for hospital purposes, and when we take into consideration all the land companies who have their share to pay and who are not here to derive any benefit, it is a very small amount among us all. I should just like to say a little about the government letting those land companies have so much vacant land; it spoils our neighborhood from getting settled up, and we have barely enough children to keep our school open. For nine straight miles south of us there is not one single person living, or one house that a hungry and cold man could get warmed up, or a bite to eat. Perhaps some of our poor returned soldiers may get some of it. I lost my oldest son in this dreadful war. I do not understand some of the women voting against the Union government, as some of them round here who did had brothers in France. Now, if you consider my letters is not worth printing, I will not be a bit offended, also, there may be a lot of misspelt words and bad grammar in it; it is a long time since I went to school. I am afraid it is very long for a first letter.

    I am yours sincerely,

                                                        H.M. Mc.

HOME LOVING HEARTS, *Free Press Prairie Farmer*
January 30, 1918

LABOR PROBLEM

Dear H.L.H.,

It is now some time since I wrote the page, but read it every week with interest, especially the editorials written by our editor, and although I am a little late, I must say a word or two on the help question that our editor spoke about. I believe it is stated the government spends upwards of forty thousand dollars bringing and securing help for farmers, but not a cent was spent for to help the farmers' wives—alas that wheat should be so dear and women so cheap! But isn't it the truth! Most women are just killing themselves with work and a big family to look after and then a lot of extra men for harvest and thrashing and a girl can't be got. I tell you I have gone through it all and now I can't stand a good day's work, and how many more are like me. Still we have to stand back while men make laws for their own good. Then I look at the nationality of the men we get, mostly all foreigners, and they are getting $4.50 a day here, and are so independent they hardly want to work for that while our poor boys are giving up their places here and going to the trenches and probably sacrificing their lives for $1.10 a day, while these aliens are demanding such a high price and enjoying all the comforts of our land. I say the government should set these men's wages at the same price as our boys are getting. Don't you think so, members? It makes me feel wild to think for they are taking our boys' places, and now as conscription is here it will get worse than ever. And another question is food economy. Every paper one picks up is "save food," and "meatless days," etc. That is all very well and I think everyone should save and even sacrifice, but is there ever a word to two "smokeless days." No, I guess there would be a rebellion right away, and they talk of us saving whole wheat bread and even a "breadless day," but still thousands and thousands of bushels of wheat, and I suppose the same amount of pounds of sugar is allowed the breweries just so the worst enemy can be made for "men" to drink. Should they be called traitors? Worse than that, and Great Britain said some time ago the liquor was their worst enemy and still men will have it. Oh! it's terrible that a civilized race of people can't do differently, but I hope the time will soon come when this terrible war is to an end, and then what a great thanksgiving there should be! But I hope we will not forget to thank the Lord for the good crops most of us have had this year, besides other blessings. Yes, I believe with some of the members that many things are wrought by prayer. I know I have been brought through a great sickness by prayer when doctors gave up, and when in trouble what a great relief and help it is to go to the Lord in prayer. You troubled ones just try it and count your many blessings to see what the Lord has done.

Could any of the members tell through the page the way to "whip" canned cream? I saw a good recipe, but have lost it.

As this letter is quite long, must say good-bye.

ILEEN

Editor's Note—Ileen will have noted that since writing, the Union government of Canada has forbidden the importation or manufacture of alcohol for the purpose of intoxicating liquors.

HOME LOVING HEARTS, *Free Press Prairie Farmer*
August 28, 1918

CHAMPIONS MARRIED WOMEN

Dear Home Loving Hearts,

I am not a subscriber, but receive the paper from a friend. I have never written to the page, but I feel as though I should like to make a few remarks. Yankee Quaker's letter was really amusing, and although, I am one of the old married women whom she says should stay at home and discharge the duties of a sensible mother. (Thank you very much for the advice. I hope you will faithfully follow it yourself. If it is ever your good luck to become one of us.) Do you suppose your remarks will have the desired effect of keeping me at home. Decidedly no! We married women can dance, and proud of the fact, but we draw the line at the Turkey trot, Bunny hug, and such disgustful dances. (By the way, where did you learn that word disgustful?) Those must be the dances that cause the numerous divorces you speak of, but a good honest dance will never give anyone cause for divorce, but in my opinion, those who get divorces, would have them if they never went to dances. The causes are generally given in private, not in public, and then again divorce is a habit with some people. You say a dance is no place for a married woman to drag a little one. When a woman is young at heart it doesn't matter what her age is. She may go to dances or where she pleases and enjoy herself, too, and it is no hardship to her or her little one either, because there can be provided a place to put the little one to sleep, and a woman doesn't need to dance till she is weary, and she can discharge her duties as a sensible mother, too. She doesn't tumble into bed as soon as she reaches home and sleep until her dinner is cooked and then get up and have breakfast and dinner together (perhaps supper too). Dear sisters, we women of the prairies have very few pleasures, only those little dances, so let us attend them all we can, and take all the children. Give them all a good time, and by the way, we are not a bit disgustful to Yankee Quaker and her like when it comes to get supper for the crowd or when there are dishes to wash. It doesn't matter whether our backs and heads ache then, and of course, if it makes her feel badly, or is disgusting to her to have us there she can stay at home.

Don't you all wish this terrible war was over? I do, and when it is what do you say to we old married people having a regular old-fashioned dance. No young people allowed. I will close now, wishing each and all of you success.

YOUNG OLD BENEDICT

HOME LOVING HEARTS, *Free Press Prairie Farmer*
August 19, 1919

TAKES ISSUE WITH FRENCHY

Dear Editor and Home Loving Hearts:

I have never written your page before, although I have read it with interest for a long time, but I could not keep from writing any longer, after seeing a letter in your issue of July 9, signed by "Frenchy." She speaks of the English bragging about their country and being palefaces living on crackers and tea. Well, "Frenchy," that is better than poor coffee and greasy water called soup that the French-Canadians I know seem to exist on, and it is one certain thing, if the English have nothing to brag about, the French-Canadians have a lot less. I know all I want to and more about French-Canadian settlements, as in order to get to my parents' home I have to stay overnight and believe me of all the times I have been there I have never had what might be called a proper clean meal, and only once has the bed been fit to sleep in, but I notice when I came to pay the bill they charged me the same as a first-class hotel. I expect the Englishmen you speak of have got in your settlement and you have got all you can from them and are now tramping on them. As to where would England be now if it wasn't for France and Belgium, I would like to know where they would be if it had not been for dear old England and her colonies. Answer that, please; and what about the money that has been and is being sent from England and Canada alone to support those suffering from war? Oh, "Frenchy," go away back and sit down.

Well, dear editor, I guess you will think I am out to write a book on it, but I will now ring off, trusting you will print this. It makes one feel sad to see the many letters in the page asking for help. Just at present I am unable to give much help, but will as soon as I can. I saw some time ago a member who said that she would be glad to make hair combings up into braids. If she is still a member and would write to me, I would gladly pay her to do some for me. I will close now with best wishes to the editor and members. I sign myself

ROSIE CHEEKED ENGLISH GIRL

HOME LOVING HEARTS, *Free Press Prairie Farmer*
November 26, 1919

DEFINITION OF A WAR BRIDE

Dear Miss Craig:

Would you be kind enough to print the following definition of an old country war bride? It may ease the minds of some poor souls who are evidently in doubt as to what the much discussed war bride really is.

A war bride is a young woman who, for some reason, appealed to the manly heart of some gallant Canadian soldier while he had the good fortune to be resident in either Scotland, England, Ireland or Wales for some period during the European war. She wears clothing, eats, drinks, sleeps and is accustomed to live in a house like other people. She has a heart and soul, which some people seem to overlook when writing on the subject to various periodicals.

She is civilized enough to feel lonesome at times and to wish that people in general would be a little more thoughtful before writing things that make her long for the dear home and parents so many weary miles away.

She is true enough woman to take her share of hardships and sorrow with the man she married and be a true companion and helpmeet to him.

The characteristics of these four types of war brides are: The English—Clever, pretty and good housekeepers. The Irish—Dainty, witty, and good cooks. Welsh—Studious, amiable and hard-working. The Scotch—Proud, mighty so.

The above refers to old country war brides only, so it is quite unnecessary for anybody to remark that I have forgotten there are just as good elsewhere, etc. I know it very well.

If any expectant mother who is having a little anxiety as to clothes for the little one on account of these dry years and poor crops, cares to write me, I will be only too happy to let her have some clothes in perfectly good condition and from a sanitary and healthy home.

"Do unto others as you would they should do unto you." With best wishes I remain

A WAR BRIDE

P.S.—My address is with Miss Craig.

HOME LOVING HEARTS, *Free Press Prairie Farmer*
December 31, 1919

CALLS ATTENTION TO LAWS

Dear Editor and Members:

I do enjoy reading the letters on H.L.H page. So many are quite helpful, and then it is like a visit to us women on the farm, that don't go out much. Keep up the good work.

Now the women surely did their share to win this war, and now that everyone is not so busy, with sewing and knitting, I want to ask the women every where to study up our laws and to work just as hard to have some of them changed, as they did to win the war. Let us women fight to have the guilty punished in such a way that others will not wish to follow in their footsteps.

Now in adultery, do you women realize how much of it is going on in our fair country? Really, we do not until we come in contact with it. Our law, that a young man who is the father of a young girl's child, should marry her or support her child is well; but sisters what about the married man that goes to his neighbors's wife and she willingly lets him in? Is there any punishment too great for them? I say "no!" Is there any punishment the man could get that would make up for the shame and disgrace and sorrow that his wife and children feel? There is no sin in this world that brings such sorrow and shame, to the true wife, as the sin of adultery. But I ask that all women take this up, all the women who read this page, and they to [sic] talk and get others, and that we petition the government to make and pass these laws:

(1) Making it a crime (with heavy punishment, not less than 15 or 20 years, at a prison farm, where they will have to work and earn their living, and help to support their wife and children), for a married man, when guilty of adultery with another man's wife or young girl. If the woman in the case is a married woman, that she be given the same punishment as the man. If a girl, old enough to know and understand that her punishment be just, the same; if very young, the court decide her case.

(2) Making it a punishable crime for any man to register falsely as man and wife in any hotel or boarding house.

(3) Making it a punishable crime for a man and woman to live together in adultery, whether they both go under the same name or different names.

The punishment for adultery should be next to that of murder.

Were public whipping the penalty for the crime of a married woman's or married man's infidelity, there would be fewer of the like scandals and ruined homes. Such a prospect of degradation, pain, shame and outraged vanity would be more effectual to kill the brute in them than all the ceremonials of courts of law. The growing immorality and reckless vice of women and men in this part of the country is terrible, and I could tell you case after case that has brought and is bringing shame and sorrow into many a home, and no punishment is given to the parties. They go a few miles away and live with some man or woman and go out to everything and have a good time; while the wife or husband, as the case may be, is left to look after the children. I know of one young woman left with five children under seven years of age, and no money; her husband away with another women. One man left three little girls, under the age of six years; his wife living with a married man, who left his wife with four children. Oh, it is time that the women's societies set up and took notice of what is going on, and not have our children so defiled. I hope the editor will kindly see fit to publish this, and I would like to come again some time.

ISABELLE

HOME LOVING HEARTS, *Free Press Prairie Farmer*
September 29, 1920

TO CAN BEEF AND PORK FOR SUMMER

Dear Editor and Home Loving Hearts:

I have enjoyed your page ever since I started taking the paper. Some letters are fine while others I don't agree with at all.

Well, harvest is about over and threshing begun, and I think most farmers will have plenty of feed for their stock this winter.

I saw "Meadow Lark" asking for the recipe for canning beef for summer and as I have a recipe thought I would write and send it to her.

Cut fresh meat in pieces about 2 inches square, sprinkle with salt and pepper to taste; mix well; pack in sealers as tight as you can; place boiler of cold water to come up almost to the top of the jars; have something in the bottom of the boiler to keep from breaking, and boil; if beef 5 hours and if pork 3 hours. Keep a kettle of boiling water on the stove and add as it boils down in the boiler. Remove jars when cooked and press meat down so that the fat and juice comes to the top of the jar. Screw lids tight and leave to get cold. This is a very handy meat for summer and is very nice. I hope this is what you want "MeadowLark."

Has any reader a good recipe for sweet tomato pickles? Can anyone send the song to the page containing these words:

"Her father is a brakie on the lonely mountain path,
   She's as gentle as the daughter of an earl,"

I would like very much to get that song.

I must get supper ready now, so hoping to see this letter in print and wishing all best wishes, I will sign myself

PEGGIE

Conclusion

Was It Worth the Journey?

By 1920 settler women were able to look back and take stock. Much of the arable prairie land was under cultivation and farmsteads were located almost every mile or so. The farms of British Columbia's interior valleys and the southern portions of Vancouver Island produced hay, vegetables, and fruits. The arid grassland areas of the three Western provinces supported large herds of cattle. Travel was easier than it had been two decades earlier because of expanded road, rail, and water systems. Most families had access to schools, churches, and medical services. In addition, women's personal and property rights were protected by law, and women had the vote.

Settlers came to the North-West for a variety of reasons. Most, however, wanted to own land. They hoped, perhaps expected, that their farms would produce endless bumper crops, fine livestock, and flourishing gardens. But as letter writers indicated, expectations often exceeded reality. Yet, in spite of setbacks, many women adapted to life on the frontier and grew to love the vast spaces and grandeur of prairie and mountains. They treasured their sense of independence, prided themselves on their self-reliance and adaptability, revelled in their role as pioneers, and took pride in their ability to create homes, rear families, and organize community activities and associations.

Other women were untrained, unprepared, and unequal to the demands of settler life. At best, rural life was difficult, and for women it was particularly demanding and stressful. Some were simply overwhelmed by events and circumstances over which they had no control. They found themselves trapped in a mire of poverty, illness, isolation, and, in some cases, abuse. Such women either moved on or lived in a bleak, hopeless state from which there seemed no escape. A third group appeared to regard themselves as survivors. They soldiered on out of duty to husbands, families, and the family business. They were worn out from hard work, childbearing, and the problems of rural life, but they appeared to cling to the dream that brought them West.

Notes to the Conclusion are on p. 153.

Dear Editor and Friends

As difficult as rural life was, parents promoted country life as the best life and the countryside as the ideal place in which to rear families. Farm wives tended to view their city cousins with jealousy and contempt, and accused city women of living a life of ease at the expense of hard-working farm women. Although concerned that their daughters and sons were attracted to urban centres, few parents appeared ready or willing to make the changes necessary to stop or at least reduce the steady flow of young people from rural areas.[1]

Settler women appeared to draw strength and courage from several sources. A number indicated that they and their husbands saw their marriages and the operation of family businesses as partnerships. These women felt needed and appreciated. Others reported that their religious faith was a constant support and succour to them. A significant number found support and direction through membership in organizations such as the Women's Institute, Women Grain Growers, or Homemakers. But the support most commonly mentioned by letter writers was the women's pages of agricultural publications. Readers perceived that both editors and writers understood the pressures and anxieties of settler life. For some readers the arrival of the women's pages was the closest thing to a visit from friends. But as communities developed so did social activities. Dramatic societies, musical groups, community dances, sports days, picnics, and quilting bees provided opportunities for people to get together.

Has time glamourized the experiences of early settlers? Do the elderly tend to recall only positive, happy, and successful events? Rasmussen, Silverman, and Heather Robertson found that settler women were anxious to tell their stories, and they related both pleasant and unpleasant memories in straightforward, dispassionate, but eloquent ways. My own visits with retired seniors or elderly family members confirm that women recall the failures, the losses, and the pain of settler life.[2] Yet they often conclude their stories with the observation that there were also good times in those bygone days. They relate amusing instances or describe how they coped through their own initiative or with the help and support of family and friends. As with letter writers, their pessimism is often juxtaposed with their optimism; next year things would be better. I believe that like these women, given the choice, my grandmother would probably go homesteading again.

In his 1905 tribute "The Women of the West," Mr. W. Fulton reminded his audience of the vital role women played in the development of Western communities. "Without her brave heart, without her strong hand and unswerving devotion to duty, what would the west be today?"[3] Letter writers not only enable me to understand and appreciate my grandmother's life, but they also provide windows into the personal lives of individual settler women almost a century ago. As the letters so clearly indicate, women not only participated in but also created history in Canada's North-West.

Notes

1 David C. Jones, "'We can't live on air all the time': Country Life and the Prairie Child," in *Studies in Childhood History: A Canadian Perspective*, ed. Patricia Rooke and R. L. Schnell (Calgary: Detselig, 1982), 185-202.

2 Bliss, "Seamless Lives," 84-100; Eliane Leslau Silverman, *The Last Best West: Women on the Alberta Frontier 1880-1930* (Montreal: Eden, 1984); Heather Robertson, *The Salt of the Earth* (Toronto: Lorimer, 1974); Rasmussen, *A Harvest Yet to Reap*; Wilfrid Eggleston, "The Old Homestead: Romance and Reality," in *The Prairie West: Historical Readings*, ed. R. Douglas Francis and Howard Palmer (Calgary: Pica Press, 1992), 339-51.

3 "The Women of the West," *Grain Growers' Guide*, June 9, 1905.

Appendix

Papers, Clubs, and Editors

Family Herald and Weekly Star

Circle of Good Company (later called Good Company)	Hostess 1896-1905 (Lilly Emily F. Barry)
Prim Rose at Home	Prim Rose 1905-

The Farmer's Advocate

Minnie May's Department   Minnie May 18??-1904

Useful information, but no letters from readers.

Ingle Nook Chats   Dame Durden 1905-
(later just Ingle Nook)

Free Press Prairie Farmer

Home Loving Hearts   Lillian Laurie 1907-1917
Home Loving Hearts   Alison Craig 1917-

The page, Woman's Work, was succeeded by Home Loving Hearts in 1906. Both pages consisted of readings, poems, fashions, and news items, but no letters from readers. When Lillian Laurie became editor in 1907, she suggested forming the Mutual Benefit Association (M.B.A.) through which readers could share ideas and information, as well as encourage and support one another. Her suggestion was well received, but only a few letters were written to the M.B.A. Women soon reverted to the title Home Loving Hearts.

Grain Growers' Guide

Mailbag

This was a regular feature. In letters to the editor both men and women aired their views on a wide range of topics, and shared information and related experiences. Letters from men predominated.

Around the Fireside   "Isobel" 190?-1911

The contents of this page was addressed to women. It included information for and letters from women.

Dear Editor and Friends

The Home   Mary Ford 1911-1912

The Home page carried items of interest as well as letters from readers.

The Country Homemakers   Francis Marion Beynon 1912-1917

The Sunshine Guild   Margaret Shields 1908-1912

The Sunshine Guild was directed to children. Shields encouraged youngsters (and adults) to join the Guild and to send their pennies, nickels, and dimes. She used the money to buy layettes for babies and clothing, books, or games for children who were very poor, in hospital, handicapped, or orphaned. Shields resigned in 1912 and Francis Marion Beynon became editor. The focus of the page quickly shifted to women's interests.

The *Grain Grower's Guide* featured a number of columns that lasted from a few weeks to a few months. These included Mothers' Experiences, The Country Mother, and Mothers' Letters.

Saturday Press and Prairie Farm

Our Welfare Page   Mrs. V. McNaughton 1916

Western Home Journal

Correspondence   No editor named

Additional Readings

Armour, Moira, and Pat Staton. *Canadian Women in History: A Chronology*. Toronto: Green Dragon Press, 1990.

Backhouse, Frances. *Women of the Yukon*. North Vancouver: White Cap Press, 1995.

Cross, Carolyn. "Adelaide Baily: Exemplary Teacher, 1857-1994." *British Columbia Historical News* 27, 2 (Fall 1994): 19-22.

Danyk, Cecilia. *Hired hands: Labour and Development of Prairie Agriculture, 1880-1935*. Toronto: McClelland and Stewart, 1995.

Fairbanks, Carol. *Prairie Women: Images in American and Canadian Fiction*. New Haven: Yale University Press, 1986.

————. "Lives of Girls and Women on the Canadian and American Prairies." *International Journal of Women's Studies* 2, 5 (1979): 452-72.

Francis, Douglas R. "In Search of a Prairie Myth: A Survey of the Intellectual and Cultural Historiography of Prairie Canada." *Journal of Canadian Studies* 24, 3 (Fall 1989): 45-67.

Gagnon, Anne. "'Our Parents Did Not Raise Us to Be Independent': The Work and Schooling of Young Franco-Albertan Women, 1890-1940. *Prairie Forum* 19, 2 (Fall 1994): 169-88.

Hak, Gordon. "Workers, Schools and Women: Some Recent Writings on the History of British Columbia." *Acadiensis* 19, 2 (Spring 1990): 185-97.

Kealey, Linda, and Joan Sangster, eds. *Beyond the Vote: Canadian Women and Politics*. Toronto: University of Toronto Press, 1989.

Kinnear, Mary, ed. *First Days, Fighting Days: Women in Manitoba History*. Regina: Canadian Plains Research Centre, 1987.

Kinnear, Mary. "Post-suffrage Prairie Politics: Women Candidates in Winnipeg Municipal Elections, 1918-1938." *Prairie Forum* 16, 1 (Spring 1991): 41-58.

Lesoway, Marie. "Women in Three Households." In Manoly R. Lupal, ed., *Continuity and Change: The Cultural Life of Alberta's First Ukrainians*. Edmonton: University of Alberta, 1985.

Light, Beth, and Ruth Roach Pierson. *No Easy Road: Women in Canada, 1920s to 1960s*. Toronto: Hogtown Press, 1990.

Lindstrom-Best, Varpu. *Defiant Sisters: A Social History of Finnish Immigrant Women in Canada*. Toronto: Multicultural History Society of Ontario, 1988.

McCallum, Margaret. *Prairie Women and the Struggle for Dower Law, 1905-1920*. Winnipeg: University of Manitoba, Canadian Legal History Project, 1992.

McFadden, Eileen. "Coeducation in the Rural West: Brandon College, 1880-1920." In Agnes Grant, Beth Westfall, and Bonnie Proven, eds., *Learning Women: A Collection of Essays*, pp. 11-23. Brandon: Brandon University Status of Women, 1990.

McPherson, Kathryn. "The Country Is a Stern Nurse: The United Rural Women, Urban Hospitals and the Creation of a Western Canadian Nursing Force 1920-1940." *Prairie Forum* 20, 2 (Fall 1995): 175-206.

Palmer, Tamara. "Ethnic Response to the Canadian Prairie, 1900-1950: A Literary Perspective on Perceptions of the Physical and Social Environment." *Prairie Forum* 12, 1 (Spring 1987): 49-73.

Pearson, Nelda K. "Women's Leadership Styles and Empowerment: A Case Study of a Canada Farm Women's Movement." *The International Journal of Canadian Studies* 11 (Spring 1995): 83-100.

Powell, Barbara. "The Diaries of the Crease Family Women." *B.C. Studies* 105/106 (Spring/Summer 1995): 45-58.

Schneider, Elise. "Addressing the Issues: Two Women's Groups in Edmonton, 1905-1916." *Alberta History* 36, 3 (Summer 1988): 16-22.

Sundberg, Sara Brooks. "A Female Frontier: Manitoba Farm Women in 1922." *Prairie Forum* 16, 2 (Fall 1991): 185-205.

Szychter, Gwen. "Women's Role in Early Farming in British Columbia." *British Columbia Historical News* 24, 1 (1990-91): 22-25.

Wells, Ronald, ed., "Letters from a Young Emigrant in Manitoba." *Prairie Forum* 8, 2 (1983).

Zilm, Glennis, and Ethel Warbinek. "Health Care Changes in the Early 1900s." *British Columbia Historical News* 20, 1 (Winter 1995-96): 8-14.

Index

Books in the Life Writing Series Published by Wilfrid Laurier University Press

Haven't Any News: Ruby's Letters from the Fifties
Edited by Edna Staebler
with an Afterword by Marlene Kadar
1995 / x + 165 pp. / ISBN 0-88920-248-6

"I Want to Join Your Club": Letters from Rural Children, 1900-1920
Edited by Norah L. Lewis
with a Preface by Neil Sutherland
1996 / xii + 250 pp. (30 b&w photos) / ISBN 0-88920-260-5

And Peace Never Came
Elisabeth M. Raab
with Historical Notes by Marlene Kadar
1996 / x + 196 pp. (12 b&w photos, map) / ISBN 0-88920-281-8

Dear Editor and Friends: Letters from Rural Women of the North-West, 1900-1920
Edited by Norah L. Lewis
1998 / xvi + 166 pp. (20 b&w photos) / ISBN 0-88920-287-7